Voodoo
Past and Present

D0807526

Louisiana Life Series, No. 5

Voodoo
Past and Present

by Ron Bodin

The Center for Louisiana Studies
University of Southwestern Louisiana

Library of Congress Catalog Number: 90-82516
ISBN Number: 0-940984-60-1

University of Southwestern Louisiana
Lafayette, Louisiana

To Patricia Rickels
and
George and Edlay Bodin

TABLE OF CONTENTS

Voodoo is Alive!

Voodoo is a red gris-gris bag the size of a small sack of marbles tossed under the front steps leading into your house by that eccentric busybody you crossed words with last week. Voodoo is a curse that once placed on its victim robs away free will, numbs the intellect, and tortures or even kills.

Voodoo conjures up images of zombis and witches, satanism, black magic and primeval tribal dance undulations—a series of images probably introduced by TV and motion pictures. To many, Voodoo is an ill-defined, cloudy, primitive kind of force the thought of which frightens us out of our pants remarkably akin to the quick rush of terror experienced when by accident we step on a slimy grass snake slivering underfoot.

Voodoo is—well, it may be whatever you have been indoctrinated to believe it to be.

We do not necessarily understand the term Voodoo or the religion it denotes, but then some things are too frightening to face—or so we may think before we actually face the feared object and exorcise its power by coming to terms with it—dissecting it, understanding it, making sense of it. This journey into Louisiana Voodoo will introduce the belief's African religious roots, the factors shaping it in the New World, news accounts of the practice seen in print since the 1840s, and will discuss many, and interview two, of Voodoo's colorful practitioners. A survey, this work seeks to familiarize the reader with the history of Voodoo and will shed new light on the rural Hoodoo of South Louisiana.

Voodoo: A Definitional Starting Point

Dictionaries define Voodoo as a religion originating in Africa as a form of ancestor worship, practiced chiefly by the Negroes of Haiti and to some lesser extent by people in other West Indian islands and in the United States. It is characterized by propitiatory rites and the use of a trance as a means of communicating with animistic dieties.[1]

In Louisiana, the Voodoo priestess Ava Kay Jones defines Voodoo as an organized religion combining elements of African Vodun and Roman Catholicism—revering the spirit world of ancestors and designed to both heal the sick and injured body as well as to guide the spirit to God.

In the rural areas of the state, a practitioner, who has introduced me to local beliefs, contends that there is no Voodoo practiced in Southwest Louisiana. Instead, Hoodoo, a series of superstitions based on a strongly

1

held belief system of Christian faith healing, characterizes the area's practices.

But no definition can capture the essence of so complex a religion as Voodoo. No definition can explain why these beliefs persist in a modern, educated world. No definition explains the reaction of colleagues when I mentioned my research. "Stay away from it," was one response. "Please don't get involved . . . it's a diabolical thing," was an English professor's admonition.

This work will attempt to shed light on Voodoo, and, in the process, I think the reader will become (like me) more amused than frightened—more respectful of other's beliefs than disdainful of simple ways—more versed in a quaint view of the world that is held by peoples of various socio-economic classes, races, and creeds.

So welcome to the world of Voodoo and to a sample of its recipes for life.

Louisiana Voodoo Recipes

How To Get A Man/Woman To Love You
Prick a finger with a pin. Put a drop of your blood on a stick of chewing gum. If the person chews the gum, he/she will not be able to resist you.
(Elizabeth Brandon)

To Harm An Enemy
Place the name of your enemy on a slip of paper and place it in the mouth of a snake. Hang the snake out in the sun to dry. As the snake suffers, so does your enemy. If the snake dies, your enemy will meet the same fate.
(Marie Laveau)

How To Obtain Unlimited Power
Tug at the clothes of a Catholic priest and the powers of the gods will be at your disposal.
(New Iberia Informant and Practitioner)

To Protect Your Health
Tie a cord that has 3, 7, or 9 knots around your waist for overall protection. Tie the cord around any part of your anatomy you want protected. After having suffered an injury, tie the cord around the injured part of your body and when the string breaks, you will be healed.
(New Iberia Informant)

For A Favor From God

Light a candle and say the following prayer: "May this offering, I pray Thee, O Lord, both loose the bonds of my sins, and win the gift of Thy Blessed Mercy." Insert your request.

(The Historic New Orleans Collection Archives)

A Cure-All

Sip a brew of Jamestown weed, sulphur, and honey from a glass which has been rubbed against a black cat with one white foot.

(R. Bourque, Lafayette)

To Protect Yourself From Spells: A Counter Agent

Walk around the house with a lighted blessed candle or throw salt into the corners of each room of your house. The process will uncross most spells.

(Elizabeth Brandon)

To Bring Money Into The House For 7 Days

Mix brown sugar, cinnamon and ammonia. Mop your floor with it, starting at the front and ending at the back. Wipe your doorknobs with ammonia and dump it out the back.

New Orleans *Times Picayune*, 16 August 1988

For A Curse That Only You Can Remove

Use a black candle, the 3 of Spades and a Voodoo doll. Utter the curse as you place your victim's likeness on the doll. Burn the black candle and place the 3 of Spades face up on the doll.

(New Iberia Informant)

For Love

Burn a blue candle lighted by 7 matches. To get love from the person you desire, light the candle daily and sprinkle Van Van oil for 9 days on the lighted blue candle.

(New Iberia Informant)

To Shorten One's Life

Wave a broom over a person's body to shorten their lifespan.

From the *Gumbo Ya Ya*
1937   Collection

For Good Luck in Gambling

Have a feather waved in your face. (As the feather waves) both you and the person waving the feather ask the gods for good luck in gambling.

For An Immediate Proposal of Marriage

Tie a rooster under the desired person's porch; seat the person in a rocking chair right over the fowl; sit beside the person and wait.

A Wishing Fetish

Cut a round piece of leather and make a bag of it. In this place 13 pennies, 9 cotton seeds, and a bit of hair from a black hog. Rub the bag whenever you want a wish to come true.

To Get Rid of a Neighbor

Kill a black chicken and throw it over the neighbor's house

To Make a Love Powder

Gut live hummingbirds. Dry the heart and powder it. Sprinkle the powder on the person you desire.

To Keep a Lover Faithful

Write the person's name on a piece of paper and put it up the chimney. Pray to it three times a day.

Gris-Gris for a Successful Marriage

Join the hands of two dolls with a ribbon. Take some sand and pile it up in a mound. On top of this place nine wax candles, sprinkle the whole with champagne saying, "St. Joseph, make this marriage and I'll pay." When the marriage takes place, put a plate of macaroni sprinkled with parsley near a tree in Congo Square in payment.

A Final Suggestion: Keep a frizzly chicken around you at all times. If someone Hoodoos you, the chicken will dig up the conjo.

West African Animism and the Birth of Louisiana Voodoo

Slave ships, floating hellholes scooped up an angry, confused, unwilling human cargo from the African continent and transported a proud people to a life of servitude in the New World. Amidst the wails, the torment, the death that accompanied such voyages, the uprooted and powerless African could no longer shape his own future. Ironic, for in Africa, especially in West Africa, the home of most early Haitian and Louisiana slaves, one seldom felt helpless or hopeless. West Africa was Animist! In the West African view of things man lived and man died—that was natural. In the natural order of things, the trees, the animals, too, were born and died. Yet death was not seen as the end of life, for life was a continuum and after death, man's spirit, his "ghost" (if he had lived a caring, decent life) remained close by loved ones—caring, assisting, and helping meet their needs.

Since man had doubles, each animate and inanimate object in nature did too. This world of "spirit-doubles" was revered by the West African. In times of need, individuals called upon their ancestors for assistance; rootmen were sought out to heal man's physical ails; and some bent on harming others called upon the vagrant, errant spirits of the damned to do their bidding.

Despite linguistic differences and antagonistic cultures, this basic world-view existed in various parts of West Africa.[2] Niles Puckett in his 1926 work, *Folk Beliefs of the Southern Negro*, writes that throughout West Africa there existed a rich "imaginary environment of ghosts and spirits." This spirit world was dominated by a supreme god. But god, being a busy god, was occupied with matters of cosmic importance. Man's needs, then, could most effectively be communicated to the supreme diety by *loas* (ancient African sub-dieties)—intermediaries who carried man's messages to the supreme godhead. Each of these *loas* had a name, possessed physical traits, had favorite foods and drinks, was represented by specific colors, possessed unique powers, and human devotees who appeased and pleased the *loa* took on characteristic behaviors associated with that messenger-god. For example, Legdea, described in later years as a handsome old man with a red flaming beard, favored meats and alcoholic drinks, was associated with the colors black and yellow, guarded crossroads and barriers, and when possessed by the *loa* (to obtain his protection) the human limped, carried a cane, and walked carefully[3]

5

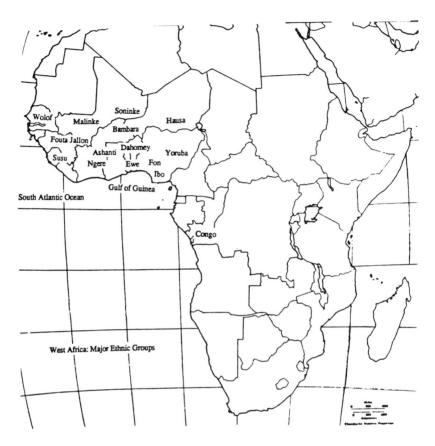

The major ethnic groups of West Africa.

It's important to remember that to the West African Animist, nature and spirit were one. And as such man needed to know about the gods so as to protect himself from spiritual or catastrophic harm and about nature's herbs and remedies to protect day-to-day health.

Interestingly, unlike the European's ghost, not all West African spirits were of a human origin, for, it will be remembered, in a traditional West African view, any person, place or thing possessed a "ghost" and this double could, by appropriate rites (prayers, chants, ceremonies), be centered in nearly any object. Preferred objects were those that had unusual qualities to them—distinctive odors, shapes and sizes. The limb of a tree that had grown into another limb was especially prized for its "doubling" and was believed to make a powerful talisman. Thus possessing this object endowed the bearer with the powers one often associates with a charm. Likewise humans could be powerful healers and magicians. Those with special powers were recognized by their unique physical features—an extra finger, facial folds, different colored eyes. Twins were especially endowed with nature's special powers. With special access to the varied array of spirits, these special people could be forces either for good or for bad.[4]

Since the "ghosts" were at man's disposal, they (and the charms they empowered) were neither innately good nor bad, but they could be utilized to improve life or to exact harm on others depending on the human user's desire.

Animism provided a simple, relatively non-ritualistic religion and world- view to people (from Senegal, the Ivory Coast, Nigeria, The Congo, Dahomey, and other West African nations) living close to the land and in close-knit family units.

The Haitian Experience

Facts about Haiti. Columbus discovered the West Indies island of Hispañola and claimed it for Spain in 1492. The first French settlers on the island were pirates who used the island as a base of operations. Spain recognized French rule of the western part of the island in 1697 under terms of the Treaty of Ryswick and the French called this western half of the island, Saint-Domingue. Slaves were transported from Africa to the island to tend the French plantations, and beginning in 1769 a series of slave revolts rocked the island leading to a general slave revolt and freedom in 1791. A former slave and foremost rebel leader, Toussaint L'Ouverture, seized the island in 1801 and proclaimed himself governor for life. Imprisoned by the

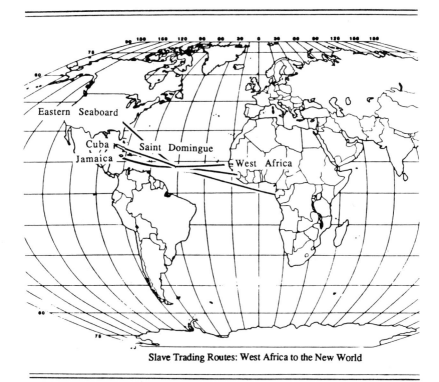

Slave Trading Routes: West Africa to the New World

French, Toussaint's generals took up the fight and won independence for Haiti in 1804.

Captivity changes man—it cages man—it brings out the survival instinct. Slavery, that great crime against human freedom and dignity, altered Vodu's enslaved African faithful and the faith itself. Slavery organized the captives into church-like cults determined to use the powers of their religion to win their freedom.

Although slaves from many African countries were transported to Haitian plantations, most of the slave population was from the Slave Coast of West Africa and consisted of peoples from the Gulf of Benin, Angola, Dahomey, and Nigeria. Throughout this region the term "Vodu" referred to any of the gods and had years of historical record. The introduction of Voodoo into Haiti may well have begun with the first group of these slaves brought to the island in the second half of the seventeenth century.[5]

In 1729, it's important to note, the Dahomey of West Africa smashed their neighbors, the snake-worshipping Ewe of Wydah and Andra and turned the two areas into a sort of slave emporium.[6] In order to obtain goods from Europeans, the Dahomey even sold their own criminals and other outcasts into slavery.

The Dahomey religion, filled with a multitude of gods and divine beings (ancestors of clans, gods of vassal tribes, and the major gods of the religion), used music as a channel for communicating with the dieties, and represented the gods by use of fetishes (praying to stones, plants, vases, bits of iron and other symbols)—this religion is strikingly similar to Haitian Vodun and Louisiana Voodoo.

Slave ships destined for Haiti housed all classes of Dahomey society and the "Vodu" religion was transported to the New World by believers and by priests on board who knew the religion's rites. [7]

Other West African slaves would contribute to the development of Voodoo in Haiti. The Ewe, for example, sold by the Dahomey into slavery, were snake-worshippers and their influence would be seen in the evolving Haitian (and later Louisiana Voodoo experience). Yet, it seems the Dahomey priests played the central role in teaching subsequent generations the names and charcteristics of the gods and the sacrifices they required.

The Dahomey "Vodu" religion, and the common worldview—the Animist worldview shared by West African people—took root and flourished in Haiti as slaves met clandestinely in night gatherings to socialize and to conspire openly under the cover of religious assemblages designed by masters to introduce the slave to Christianity.

With few Catholic priests to lead slave religious instruction and worship, the Vodu priest often assumed that role and substituted African practices. Slaves met, plotted runaway schemes, and generally exchanged ideas, and in the process, kept their religion alive much like secret orders have maintained taboo ways and beliefs throughout man's history.

So important and pervasive was the Dahomey influence that within a generation of the first slaves arrival in Haiti, Vodu priests had been successful at developing temples, organizing clergy, and maintaining ritual "Vodu" dances in the new slave environment of Haiti and under the less than watchful eye of Spanish-Catholic authorities.[8]

The "Vodu" influence in Haiti even played a role in the island's numerous slave uprisings. Macadal in 1757 led a fanatic band of fugitive slaves assuring his followers that the gods would not permit their recapture and promising immortality and protection from bullets. Romaine in 1793 claimed to be the godchild of the Virgin Mary and convinced his "troops" of their "Vodu" invincibility and campaigned to poison masters and their livestock in an attempt to win slave freedom. Hyacinthe, who distinguished himself at the Battle of Croix des Bouquets, feared no cannon and had his troops blessed for protection by both Catholic and "Vodu" priests. [9]

With the start of the nineteenth-century the long awaited Haitian slave revolution witnessed a new stage in the development of "Vodu." African Vodu cults were a unifying force that were used to the advantage of the revolutionaries especially when "Vodu" priests enthusiastically inspired their followers—now black soldiers—into political associations determined to win slave freedom. "Vodu" ceremonies in Haiti provided slave solidarity—members felt like family, embued the intitiated with confidence of spirit protection—the Vodu ghosts being summoned to cast away all harm from the combatants, and assured secrecy—members understood that to disclose secrets of Vodu was to blaspheme god himself.[10] As Vodu organized and motivated the black to fight colonial oppression, the cult itself became more organized and ritualistic and hierarchical.

So the basic African-inspired Haitian rituals of the 1730's incorporating simple ceremonies—a snake, a dance, a few convulsions—evolved into an organized religion in Haiti. Haitian Voodoo, asserting that man possessed two spirits—the *Gros Bon Ange,* that animated the body, and the *Ti-Z-Ange,* that protected against danger day and night, had assisted Haitian revolutionaries in their recruiting and fighting, and in turn had been used by these revolutionaries for their own purposes—leading to further religious synthesis. With the end of the Revolution, blacks had achieved victory (the revolutionary's reward) and the Vodu religion too benefited from the struggle as it emerged an organized and formidable force in Haitian life.[11]

Louisiana, like Haiti, had also been ruled and misruled and ignored by both the French and the Spanish. A humid, bug and disease-infested environment greeted settlers to the the lower Mississippi Valley and with relatively few Europeans willing to move to the area, slaves were imported into the Louisiana colony in ever-increasing numbers to clear the area and to work plantations, and these slaves were primarily from West Africa.

The Haiti-Louisiana Connection

For some years there had been movement of slaveowners and slaves between Haiti and New Orleans, but in 1809 a large number of Haitian planters who had refugeed in Cuba during Touissant L'Ouverture's Haitian revolution, were expelled from Cuba and, with their slaves, made their way to New Orleans. Many of the slaves accompanying these planters were snake worshippers and devotees of "Vodu."[12]

In such a way, significant numbers of Haitian slaves came to Louisiana. In the past, reports of West Indies slaves poisoning masters had in part motivated a banning on such "unreliable and rebellious slaves" from Louisiana. But with the arrival of the Haitian refugees and their slaves, this ban was of little useful consequence since the Louisiana slave came into routine contact with the feared Haitian slave at plantations that "housed" working slaves from many parts of Africa, at clandestine nighttime "sings," and in the cities where some slaves worked and where rural slaves were able to visit. With the United States purchase of Louisiana in 1803 owners continued to press for the importation of slaves and the ban remained unenforceable and increased numbers of West Indies slaves entered Louisiana from Haiti and slave traders continued importing these slaves from Jamaica via Pensacola, from Kentucky, Virginia and various other places.[13] So a considerable Haitian slave presence was felt in Louisiana, and these slaves were known to practice various African and Haitian "Vodu" rites.

Louisiana possessed a unique culture, a unique environment. In this very different world emerged a unique brand of Voodoo—less organized than the

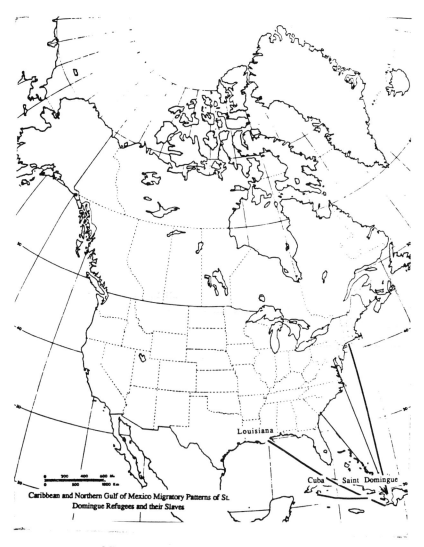

Migratory Patterns of St. Domingue Refugees
and Their Slaves

Haitian model, influenced by the mysteries of Catholicism and the basic beliefs of European superstition, and business-oriented.

The Louisiana Slave Influence

Available records seem to indicate that most Louisiana slaves were from the African Slave Coast—originally residing in the area of the Senegal, Gambia, and Niger rivers.[14] Through a French slave-trading company, a subsidiary of the Company of the Indies, these Senegambian, Bandara, and Mandigo peoples were sold to Louisiana planters and farmers, bringing with them religious traditions of faith-healing and their own brand of Voodoo. Many slaves, however, native to other regions of Africa were also transported to Louisiana. Sharing a similar worldview, these different peoples held in common a belief system rooted in the conviction that one's welfare depends on understanding the complexities of gods, spirits, and ancestors.[15] This belief system was their religion, their medicine, their way of protecting themselves from diseases of all kinds, and from death. A shared tradition of African root doctors, also known as conjurers, or hoodoomen had status in each of these cultures and the practitoners' knowledge of herbal remedies was integrated with the ritual skills of devination (reading the future) and magic (the casting of spells). Thus it appears that some slaves in Louisiana had practiced Voodoo-like ways in Africa and came to practice a form of Louisiana Voodoo long before born in Africa and modified by many forces including the influence of the "visiting" slaves from Haiti.[16]

Louisiana: A Unique Milieu for the Development of Voodoo

Niles Puckett seems to accept this view and asserts that from his interviews in the early part of the twentieth century with former slaves and slave-holders further evidence emerges of a unique milieu for the development of a distinct brand of Louisiana Voodoo.[17] Contrary to popular notion, since slave owners had an economic stake in the health of their "chattel," it was not unknown for a Louisiana owner to provide medical care for his slaves. Some owners contracted with physicians for routine visits to the slave quarters (though most care was much less systematic and based on the economic bottom line). Other owners provided yearly physical examinations for the plantation's slaves. Some owners transported slaves to doctors on an as-needed basis. Owners considered preventive health maintenance a simple matter of economy—it made good business sense to protect one's investment. A sick slave could not work or could not work as efficiently as desired. And a dead slave represented a total loss on the owner's financial investment.

This "care" extended to protecting the slave from physical injury at the hands of any other bondman. A slave was not permitted to do injury to another of the owner's slaves. Slaves were forbidden from striking, molesting, or killing other thralls. In the absence of any available means for retaliation, the slave fell back on this African heritage and on the Haitian slave model present in Louisiana since at least 1809, and utilized Voodoo as one way of getting back at fellow slaves for wrongs real and imagined.[18]

The West African slave against all odds seems to have maintained his pride (often being accused of being arrogant by some white slaveowners), his determination to be free and most importantly, some of his traditional ways in an alien and forbidding atmosphere.[19] Recall that in Haiti many of the slave uprisings were led by "Vodu" practitioners who deeply believed that the magic of the spirits made them invincible.[20] This conservation of basic culture—never completely abandoning one's past ways and beliefs— especially those Voodoo beliefs that empowered one in a world where the slave could not control his destiny—existed throughout the area; coupled with distinctive synthetic features of the slave experience (including the deliberate intermingling of many African peoples speaking differing languages on one plantation so as to divide and conquer the African—the oppressive slave-work environment and the resultant need for the slaves to preserve as much of their individuality as possible under the circumstances) this cultural conservatism helps explain the melding of the many African "Vodu" rites (practiced by slaves from different African tribes) into a unique Louisiana Voodoo intended to bring people together in the face of a common enemy, the slaveholder.[21]

Of even greater significance to the development of an indigenous Louisiana Voodoo was the fact that slaves had some opportunity to practice and keep alive their traditional Animist ways even in the slave "encampment".[22] This was possible since a number of slave owners either did not care about the slave's "savage" private practices or toleratred those practices that did not interfere with the work schedule. Some owners even allowed slaves off the premises by issuing passes as long as the slave and livestock used as transportation were fresh for the next work day. It should also be remembered that slaveowners were not a monolithic group, and various owners displayed a range of tolerance for slave recreational activity. For economic reasons some owners allowed slaves to travel on weekends thereby freeing the owner from feeding the slaves for that period of time.

Some owners allowed slaves to cultivate small gardens in wooded areas to reduce owner expenses especially during hard economic times—thus providing added opportunity for slave movement and slave meetings. The opportunites provided to slaves (in Louisiana) by such an array of factors permitted much intraslave contact and helps explain the development of a new synthetic culture for blacks—one needed by second and third generation slaves (a race now without a country or an identity) and with little remaining formal knowledge of their African heritage.[23]

Additionally, in Louisiana the French colonial government's Black Code had guaranteed basic slave rights including minimum clothing and nutrition standards, some basic familial rights, an obligation to provide for the slave's spiritual needs, slave rights to petition courts for redress and to be tried for major offenses, and restrictions on physical and sexual abuse. Although compliance with these regulations was voluntary, French settlers, unaccustomed to slavery and to the control of slaves, by and large heeded the regulations especially early in the slave experience and they especially abided by those regulations convenient in helping manage the slave.[24] This compliance served to ameliorate the abuses one often associates with American slavery and, together with the "free time" opportunites afforded, aided the Louisiana slave in maintaining some semblance of personal freedom. For to the African "spirits," herbs, and nature were all tied into one's sense of personal freedom, and were used for health and as an exercise in personal liberty.

Some find it amazing that slaves were allowed free time. But in fact, time away from the plantation routine was usually provided on Sundays, on holidays, from sundown to sunup, and on Saturday afternoons. During the Christmas holidays some slaves (especially the owner's household servants) were dealt with paternalistically, being provided new clothes and allowed to attend balls hosted on a rotating basis at various slave quarters. This movement off the slaveholder's grounds is also sometimes seen on Sundays when the slave was allowed to attend a church (a segregated white church or a slave camp meeting). Despite white patrols intended to curb any such freedom of slave movement, it has been noted that slaves did leave the master's grounds and used the information gathered on such forays and their wits to "temporarily escape" at any given chance to other slave quarters and to the countryside, or to the city, for a few hours of respite and recreation with fellow slaves.[25]

Slaves participating in voodoo dances.
(Courtesy of The Historic New Orleans Collection)

Slave dancers in Congo Square, New Orleans.
(Courtesy of The Historic New Orleans Collection)

Even before the "Christianization" of the African slave, a favored slave recreational and communal activity, nightime services and "sings" took place in slave cabins with large iron pots placed on the floor to absorb the noise of the goings on, or in remote areas of the owner's landholdings late at night and often without the slaveowner's knowledge.[26] At times services were held in an arbor church of canvas or netting stretched over a wooden frame that was attached to "sacred trees" that (Animist) slaves felt possessed powers derived from their unique looks or configurations. Slaves from several plantations often met weekly with or without permission "to sing, pray, and get happy."[27] With the passage of time, and a change in slave-owner sentiment, partially explained by the owner's perception of increased slave thievery, runaways, and a thwarted 1748 slave revolt, slaveholders in Louisiana became increasingly harsh in treating slave misbehavior, and initiated a futile drive to curb slave movement and assemblage.

In cities, slaves congregated at dances and in "tin pan alleys" in such numbers that by 1817 the New Orleans City Council saw fit·to set aside for purposes of crowd control and illicit blackmarket activity control (an illicit trade had developed flamed by slave thefts from the master's properties and sales of these goods to intermediaries in the back alleys of cities) a place for slaves to openly congregate (and trade, entertain themselves with "tribal songs" and dance under the watchful eye of the authorities)—an area located across from Rampart Street and known as Congo Square (the currrent site of the Louis Armstrong Park).[28] These dances were witnessed by whites and years later the dances were written about by Schulz, Latrobe, and Lafcadio Hearn among others. These dances, at first simple affairs accompanied by homemade musical instruments playing distinctive African numbers, by the middle of the nineteenth century had developed into an African-American mode, and early on were seen not only in New Orleans but also on various Louisiana plantations.[29]

Some slaves appear to have used these various "recreational" times to see conjurers in order to "make masters kind, to insure love, to harm enemies and to heal the sick."[30] That the slave did so comes as no surprise, since their traditional culture had for generations made use of the root-man, the conjurer. Some slaves seem to have used the opportunity to exert control over fellow slaves by use of the "magical" powers connected with Voodoo. A gris-gris strategically placed gave the self-proclaimed, but otherwise economically and politically powerless Voodoo practitioner, control over those who either feared or respected the ways of Voodoo. Other slaves utilized meetings as the basis for communal experience and group identification, and this communal experience would be the basis for an emerging and close-knit black church.[31]

Voodoo represented one of the few ways for blacks to gain economic and personal power in a racist and chauvinistic world. A number of blacks discovered this reality and thus started the business of Voodoo in Louisiana.

The Rise of Organized Voodoo

After the Civil War and with emancipation, the former slave fended for himself, and the treatment of diseases was back in the hands of the recently freed slave. Believing that a mule and forty acres would be forthcoming, some former slaves waited for a better day. When that largesse failed to materialize, the former slave could either opt to journey north for employment or could seek contractual employment or hired-hand status with the former master. A constant need to make do with scarce funds soon "focused attention again on the all-powerful 'root doctor' or 'hoo-doo' man as a healer of diseases.[32] This return to African tradition also helped shape nineteenth-century Louisiana Voodoo—a Voodoo that evolved close-knit, anti-white features in reaction first to slavery and then to the emerging Jim Crow mentality that witnessed whites substituting hatred of blacks for pre-Civil War pity of the race. Under these circumstances Voodoo became more organized over the years and less Africanized in the context of the ever-changing Louisiana black experience.

By the late nineteenth and early twentieth centuries, a number of chroniclers (including H. C. Castellanos, Marie Dana, S. Cullen, W. H. Seymour, Mary A. Owens and others) reported on the existence of a New Orleans Voodoo society now apparently so tightly organized as to constitute an order of sorts.[33]

The Rise of Voodoo Kings and Queens and Voodoo Ceremonies in New Orleans

This secret society's "rituals" were a colorful affair. Members changed clothes prior to the ceremonies putting on sandals, and girdling their loins with red handkerchiefs. The queen was attired in red and wore a red sash. But most splendidly dressed was the king who wore a great number of colorful handkerchiefs, boasted a blue waist cord and "red stuff" on his head.[34]

Reports of this society's meetings were remarkably similar. As had been the case with the slaves' "sings" and socials, secret Voodoo meetings

Reports of this society's meetings were remarkably similar. As had been the case with the slaves' "sings" and socials, secret Voodoo meetings were also held at night, but now were formally structured and were presided over by a king and queen. The queen was the dominant figure at the ceremony and was elected to her position for life (the king was often her husband). The meetings were started with the adoration of a snake placed in a barred cage or on an altar positioned in front of the king and queen. Next came the renewal of the society's oath of secrecy. Often the king and queen extolled future happiness and exhorted subjects always to seek their advice. So powerful an influence was the queen that believers were often reminded that to break with her was to break with the gods themselves. At that point in the ceremony, individual members came up to implore the Voodoo god, to invoke blessings on loved ones, and curses on enemies. All the while, the king listened patiently until the "spirit" moved him. Thereupon he would quickly place the queen on the ornate box containing the snake oracle. Simultaneous to her seating on the box containing the oracle or soon afterwards, the queen convulsed and talked through "spirit lips" in an unknown tongue. An offering was taken up. And throughout the course of the ritual, tafia, an intoxicating mixture akin to rum, was consumed heightening the effects of the ceremony. Then the much anticipated Voodoo dance followed the initiation of new candidates to the order. As the ceremony began, the king traced a large circle in the center of the room with a piece of charcoal and placed the neophyte in the drawn circle. The candidate's head was sprinkled with herbs, horsehair, rancid tallow, and broken bits of bone. Candidates writhed, danced, and if in the process stepped out of the circle, the king and queen hurriedly turned their backs to the initiate in order to neutralize this bad omen. Finally, the candidate took his lifetime oath; the king struck him lightly on the head with a wooden paddle; then the entire assemblage got the "spirit" and broke into convulsive dance as the ritual snake was passed from participant to participant.[35]

This colorful and often feared Voodoo society may have been the most open under the "reign" of the last great Voodoo queen, Marie Laveau, who died in 1881 at the age of eighty-five.[36]

Marie Laveau—Voodoo Queen

Laveau was a free person of color. Church records indicate she married Jacques Paris, a free black, in 1819 at ceremonies officiated at by the

Marie Laveau and her daughter, ca. 1881.
(Courtesy of The Historic New Orleans Collection)

popular Père Antoine. Although a controversial figure steeped in lore, some consensus exists regarding Marie Laveau. For example, she was Catholic; she lived in the 1900 block of Rampart Street; her husband vanished a short time after their marriage and was presumed dead; Laveau became a hairdresser to support herself, and then lived with, and had fifteen children probably by her lover, Louis C. Duminy de Glopion, who some believe was a native of Saint-Domingue and the son of a French military officer.[37]

It is not clear how Marie Laveau actually became involved in Voodoo. An active society existed before Laveau and it is evident that the society was influenced by natives of Haiti such as the heavily tatooed and mesmerizing Dr. John, John Montenet, who some claim first blended Haitian Voodoo, Catholicism, the snake oracle, and "flim-flam"—enticing white women to his "advice parlor" with his listening skills, sure demeanor, and "magical cures."[38] The result was a mixture of African Animism, Catholic saints confused with the Voodoo gods of Africa and Haiti, and specific practices born of the practitioner's imagination.[39] It is also evident that a number of Voodoo queens "reigned" at any one time. Sanité Dédé was queen before Laveau, and one, Marie Soloppe, was coming to power when Laveau appeared on the scene as the most powerful Voodoo figure in New Orleans.[40] Perhaps Laveau's talent for the theatrical, her business acumen, and her personal charisma together with her knowledge of personal secrets acquired during her hairdressing days helped propel her to prominence.[41] In any case, Laveau's reputation eclipsed that of other queens (it is alleged that this was accomplished by a combination of brute force and the strategic use of gris-gris) making her an influential figure on the New Orleans scene. In the process, Laveau put her unique stamp on Voodoo. Claiming her followers were Christian, Marie Laveau added statues of saints, prayers, incense, and holy water to the traditonal Voodoo rites which had for some time incorporated snakes, a black cat, roosters, blood drinking, and fornication.[42]

Increasingly powerful, Laveau consistently intimidated the superstitious with her magic and politicians with the "dirt" she had gathered on them while curling the hair of the the city's wealthy white and mulatto women and listening to their gossip. For example, it has been alleged that Laveau upon hearing of one man's desire for a political job sought the aspirant out and informed him of her "knowledge," and assured him a job was "in the cards." In turn, she used her knowledge of a local politician's indescretion and blackmailed him into offering the aspirant a job. In the process, Laveau was financially reimbursed by the job seeker, and she formed a friendship with the newly employed figure, and an associaton with a fearful elected official.[43]

In addition, Laveau was known to use her knowledge of an extramarital affair to blackmail nearly any prominent New Orleans gentleman, confront his wife with the facts of the case, claim the episode's cause to be Voodoo, and obtain money from the wife for uncrossing the husband and freeing him of the other woman's clutches. She would then proceed to tell the husband of her "good deed" rescuing him from responsibility and his wife's ire, and accept another "token" of the husband's appreciation for services rendered.[44]

Enjoying her notoriety, Laveau was frequently seen at public events and "presided" in fine rainment over the calinda dances at Congo Square. Though no Voodoo ceremonies are believed to have taken place at the square, Laveau capitalized on the public's fascination with the Congo Square activities and opened up the less sensitive Voodoo ceremonies to the public (for an admission fee). She also built a home, La Maison Blanche, near Milneburg where yellow-skinned girls were believed to entertain white and black males from the New Orleans area. Voodoo, it seems, was one of the few avenues to power and economic potential for blacks. Laveau used this access to forge a better life for herself in a racist and sexist environment.[45] The bulk of Laveau's time, though, was spent at her New Orleans home on St. Anne Street carrying out the staples of her successful Voodoo enterprise, placing and removing curses, telling fortunes, and conjuring with her mix of gris-gris, Guinea Peppers in the mouth, and prayers recited in front of the St. Louis Cathedral—additional assistance she rendered for a fee.[46]

During Laveau's lifetime and for some time after her death, perhaps due to the queen's marketing skills, Voodoo became increasingly popular; especially notable was the increased participation by whites as was seen in an 1896 Voodoo festival on St. John's Eve held on Bayou St. John near New Orleans. St. John's Eve has been a special date since ancient times in Europe when pagan sun worshippers rolled blazing wheels down hills to celebrate the sun's descent. (The Louisiana mixture of African Animism, Haitian Voodoo, and European influences is seen in the adoption of this date as the highpoint in the Louisiana Voodoo calendar). Non-participating spectators reported that the 1896 New Orleans festival started with the believers building a fire. The Voodoo participants were then seen dancing, destroying a black cat, and devouring its remains. Another festival held between Spanish Fort and Milneburg was attended by large numbers of whites and the participants even served hot New Orleans coffee and Creole

THE OLD LAVEAU HOUSE.

Marie Laveau's residence.
(Courtesy of The Historic New Orleans Collection)

The banks of Bayou St. John, where voodoo ceremonies were held.
(Courtesy of The Historic New Orleans Collection)

Marie Laveau's tomb in St. Louis Cemetery, New Orleans.
(Courtesy of The Historic New Orleans Collection)

gumbo to the assembled spectators who had paid a $10 admission fee. On several occasions at such ceremonies male observers were told not to remove their jackets so as not to break the meeting's spell.[47] Nonbelievers, still these observers did not test fate and abided by the requests.

An 1860s raid on a similar event included the arrest of prominent white women, and prominent white males were identified as attending a Voodoo ceremony presided over by the Voodoo doctor Alexander.[48] So popular in fact were these ceremonies that they were eventually moved to a remote location near Lake Pontchartrain, and the ceremonies were attacked by the press especially after increased reports of white participation, as seen in a June 25, 1873, New Orleans *Daily Picayune* article, bemoaning the fact that such events could take place in a Christian community without punishment.[49]

With Emanciapation and increased economic and educational opportunities, old ways of acquiring power—especially by the use of chicken bones, clam shells, dolls and oils— were either no longer needed or no longer acceptable to those wishing to be assimilated into the mainstream of American society.

Disintegration of Voodoo Into Do-It-Yourself Superstitions

After Marie Laveau, a less open Voodoo organization emerged characterized by the use of spells, tricks, conjurations, witchcraft, and modern seances.[50] Molding a waxen heart and sticking pins in it, burning tapers with the idea that before the last taper is consumed a mysterious force will cause the wanderer to return— all elements of late nineteenth-century Louisiana Voodoo are quite medieval and very European .[51] The European influence on the constantly evolving Voodoo experience is better understood when one considers that in medieval Europe a fine line separated religion and magic. Even the Christian "faithful" were known to seek remedies for their earthly problems by "worshipping" saints who had performed miracles, by reciting prayers, and by venerating the holy altar. Paralleling the religious life of the church in medieval Europe was another belief system rooted in ancient paganism and characterized by wizards, sorcerers, charmers, conjurers, prophets, and practitioners who combined their rites with the recitation of prayers and the use of Christian charms. With the increased participation of whites in Voodoo and with the influence of New World Catholicism on practitioners, it is no surprise that in the late nineteenth century Lafcadio Hearn, a literary figure and a keen observer of cultures,

Planter using a Voodoo charm to intimidate his workers.
(Courtesy of The Historic New Orleans Collection)

claimed that the European influence had succeeded in considerably modifying African Voodoo in Louisiana.[52]

But by the 1920s it was difficult to find any trace of the once thrivng and tightly organized Voodoo society in Louisiana.[53] Some blacks seem to have turned their backs on traditional ways in an attempt to be assimilated into the dominant social structure as an avenue for personal, political, and economic power. With increased educational opportunity, the superstitious nature of the belief system may have discredited Voodoo. Simply put, there no longer was a need for an organized Voodoo in Louisiana and so the formal, structured "religion" disappeared.

Nonetheless, the fascination with Voodoo remains, but the practice has taken on a different flavor—a combination of watered-down Voodoo rituals mixed with Catholicism and often designed to do nothing more than get favors from the saints.[54] It is perhaps symbolic that ritualistic Voodoo meetings after Laveau took place out of public sight in isolated locations often where the cypress swamp behind New Orleans meets the waters of Lake Pontchartrain. A witness observed that one such affair in a fisherman's cabin was presided over by a nondescript queen who conducted a ceremony for cross-legged followers. During the ceremonies drummers beat their thumbs on gourds covered with sheepskin and old men sang as the congregation marched, drank an alcoholic concoction, and made fire blaze by spraying alcohol from the mouth and setting a candle to the flammable spray.[55] The ceremony had indeed changed since Laveau's heyday.

Since World War I it seems that a new breed of conjurer has also appeared on the Louisiana scene. In New Orleans, Mother Doris, for example, taught classes in prophesying, and healing.[56] Anxious to appeal to a different clientele, Mother Doris, like many practitioners who followed her, did not label her work Voodoo. She was a Christian and altogether de-emphasized the Voodoo rites. Practitioners such as Lula White and Julia Jackson similarly sold potions, charms, and gris-gris (and remedies), but did not openly practice ritualistic Voodoo. They did privately carry on some activities connected with the old variety of organized Voodoo. That connection to the Voodoo past is perhaps best seen in the traditional recipes practitioners developed for potions. In one recipe, Lula, infamous for her "Mahogany" Storyville brothel, taught that an enemy could be made to suffer by placing a slip of paper with the enemy's name in the mouth of a snake, and then hanging the snake out in the sun to dry. If the snake died, the enemy did too. Marie Laveau had used similar recipes. Dr. Cat, a self-proclaimed witch doctor eventually convicted of mail fraud, even went so far

as to incorporate modern notions of mail-order marketing to peddle his array
of popular potions. By the 1940s a number of storefront operations and
self-proclaimed witch doctors were all that seemed to remain of the once
thriving New Orleans Voodoo church.

Today New Orleans Voodoo is merchandised in French Quarter
boutiques; is practiced by priestesses trained in Haiti; rural Voodoo is faithbased, and transported to the city by those seeking urban employment, and
is still practiced with earnest in a few suburban establishments.

Voodoo made its way into the bayous of Southern Louisiana, but Voodoo's
formal organization did not. Rural Louisiana Hoodoo was individualistic,
faithbased, and handed down from generation to generation by word of
mouth like a good folk-tale or a traditional Cajun song.

Wealthy, well-educated planters and city people enjoyed the services of
doctors and clergy in their hour of need. They owned guns and with frontier
law on their side, employed violence to deal with human affronts and
obstacles of all kinds.

In the remote areas of the state, on the other hand, where schools and
physicians and clergy were scarce, the small farmers and ranchers—though
frontiersmen all—often felt powerless and helpless in this world and relied
on a blend of European mysticism and Christian dogma to explain life's
setbacks. Spun by a people steeped in the folktale, spells were often
believed responsible for devastated crops, and sorcery explained mysterious
and disastrous livestock epidemics (and other tragedies otherwise
inexplicable). To fight off illness, teas and prayers and religious objects
like holy water, scapulars, and oils were utilized. That's all there was. That's
what was used.

Country life was difficult. Death and misery were common. Often
there seemed little hope of ever improving one's circumstances and the
future seemed as bleak as the living one could eek out on the bayous and
prairies of Louisiana.

It's not surprising that during the first two centuries of Louisiana's
settlement, a do-it-yourself approach to religion and health care emerged and
was especially popular with the small farmers in rural Louisiana. Faith-
healers, using prayers and Catholic sacramentals, were respected practitioners
in South Louisiana who were sought out to "heal" minor illnesses. The

A Guide to New Orleans Voodoo

1. 1900 block of Rampart St., site of Marie Laveau's childhood home
2. 1020 St. Anne, site of Laveau's last home
3. Congo Park (now Armstrong Park), site of African (Calinda) dances
4. Storyville--site of brothels, later of Voodoo Queens like Lula Jackson
5. Milneburg (Pontchartrain Park)--site of Dr. John's home, and of Laveau's Maison Blanche
6. 813 Toulouse, office of the Yoruba priestess Ava Kay Jones
7. 840 Elysian Field, Lady Bishop's One Way Church of Truth
8. 730 Bourbon, Marie Laveau's Voodoo Supply Shop
9. 724 Dumanine, Historic New Orleans Voodoo Museum
10. 801 N. Broad, F & F Botanica (Supplies for various Voodoo-like faiths)
11. 5728 Fourth St.,--Sr. Susan Verdin's (Hoodoo) shop located across the Mississippi River from New Orleans in Marrero

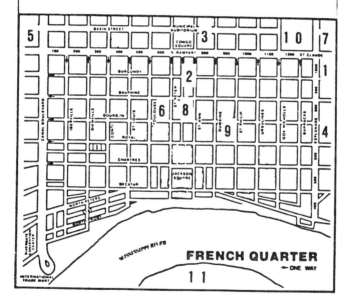

medical doctor, often residing some distance away, providing expensive care was used sparingly—mostly for treating major illnesses.[57]

But faith-healing isn't Voodoo. Perhaps European superstitions and African animism influenced rural inhabitants, but ritualistic Voodoo was never accepted by any mainstream group and was openly feared by most. So where did hoodoo, the country-cousin of Voodoo originate?

Certainly there has been a large black population in rural Louisiana since slavery days that for generations has depended on the African Animist tradition of rootmen, hoodoomen, and conjurers. Relying on nature and on a watered down, splintered version of New Orleans inspired Voodoo, blacks may well have provided one of the "ingredients" needed for the development of rural Louisiana hoodoo.

Still today Louisiana hoodoo practitioners are predominantly black, predominantly rural, and predominantly poor. Not so their clients—they represent all social classes, races, and ethnic groups. The client is often, though, desperate for assistance, revenge-obsessed, or from a home where hoodoo practitioners were routinely consulted by family members to help meet human needs.

Most white hoodoo practitioners in the area appear to have learned their craft—one that amounts to a series of individualized superstitions—from blacks or from family members. There seems to have existed a number of popular responses to rural isolation—in such a world it was acceptable to be superstitious, to practice faithhealing, to use simple sorcery; some rural blacks considered it acceptable to maintain traditional rootmen and conjurer ways.

The simple "conjurer" was and remains tolerated by blacks and whites alike. He is an individualist. He is perhaps best described as the family's black sheep. The conjurer is harmless since he relies on prayers, readings from the Bible, the burning of incense, and speaking in unknown tongues to "read" into the future, to prepare love and other potions, and to ward off evil spirits.

Little tolerance though is accorded the person who delves into Black Magic; they are feared. They have crossed the line from socially acceptable activity to behavior considered taboo. Whether they are rich or poor, black or white—these practitioners often are identified as society's outcasts— people with few or bizarre social skills—people never completely accepted by their own. Historically, hoodoo afforded these outsiders considerable status—even if it was of a negative nature—in a remote part of the country where anonymous lives were pretty much the norm. In such an environment, "Black" hoodooists were anything but anonymous. They were and remain easily identifiable by nervous neighbors who characterize the practitioners as spooky characters who you don't want to cross.

Recently, younger people in the area have violated another taboo— mixing Satanism with Voodoo-like rituals. Perhaps the addictive nature of hoodoo beliefs first reported by folklorist Elizabeth Brandon in the 1960s, like other addictions, requires constantly increased levels of stimulation to "fix" the junkie—Satanism is not Voodoo, but it seems to provide an extra surge of power to the addictive personality involved in these behaviors.

Rural Hoodoo Accounts: Prayers, Candles, and Incense— 1950-1990

It would be a mistake to suppose that no Voodoo activity remains in Louisiana (and throughout the U. S. for that matter). Puckett, in the 1920s interviewed practitioners from around the South who were actively seeking out the church—looking for a Voodoo congregation. To this date, New Orleans cemetery custodians report to the police incidents of grave "plants"—animal tongues, for example, dotted by Voodoo pins buried at gravesites hoping to tap into the powers of ghosts and spirits. Some practitioners seek out Marie Laveau's tomb hoping to tap into her powers.[58] So what has happened to Voodoo? Perhaps the organized society so associated with Laveau disintegrated (this writer's belief); perhaps it evolved into modern Voodoo superstitions; or perhaps Voodoo went deep underground.

Vermilion Parish "Conjos," Fetishes, and Gris-Gris

Nonetheless, accounts of Voodoo-like ritual, some taking on the aspects of folklore, continue to be reported throughout the state. In Vermilion Parish, a rural county in the heart of Cajun country, folklorists discovered in the 1950s that although relatively few people practiced or believed in hoodoo, many knew of conjurers and their gris-gris or "conjos." People of all social and economic stripe understood that when conjured the victim has a spell cast on him and something is bound to happen to him. It was understood that the conjurer's charms have the power to attract love, protect from diseases, induce pleasant dreams, assure gambling luck, torment or even kill an enemy. There was evidence that a tiny number of whites and blacks, Protestants and Catholics, literate and illiterate, poor and wealthy were addicted to these beliefs.[59]

Vermilion Parish informants also provided information on the use of good luck charms that were carried in pockets or sewn into clothing or worn around the neck or the waist. Even as late as the 1950s people knew that malevolent charms could be hidden in closets, pillows, drawers, dark corners, under mattresses and beds, and outside in flower beds and shrubbery or close to or under doorways.[60]

An Abbeville resident provided an amazing account of her entire home being hoodooed. While residing in the dreaded house she reported that once her curtains caught fire spontaneously, that food would routinely disappear from the dinner table as soon as she set it out, and that her children's clothes would disappear from their closets. Finally her family decided to leave the house, but after another family tried to inhabit the house and experienced the same hoodoo experiences, they too moved out and the house was subsequently abandoned.[61]

A number of Vermilion Parish informants were also able to report on the recipes for these hoodoo fetishes that cause such mischief. Some were made from alligator teeth, grains of plants, cords with 3, 7, or 9 knots, or were contained in little bags of red flannel filled with so-called magic substances including nail-clippings, feathers, human or animal hair, dried nerves from the wings of a vulture, snake bones, powdered dried snakeskin, dirt or dust collected at cemeteries, and some strong smelling items— mustard grains, asafetida or garlic.

Some informants also knew of less complicated gris-gris often in the form of conjured food put in front of a victim, and of victims becoming crazy or possessed after eating the food. These various charms could be purchased from a hoodooman or if one knew the recipe, could be "cooked up." Amazingly, many of the ingredients were available at local pharmacies and groceries.[62]

To counteract the gris-gris, Vermilion Parish informants suggested a number of counteragents. One suggested technique involved walking around the house with a lighted blessed candle or throwing salt in the corners of each room where the suspect had been.

A number of Vermilion Parish informants knew of hoodoo practices and of people who had used hoodoo, but stressed that they did not themselves practice the rites. For example, Henry Saltzman of Gueydan informed folklorist Elizabeth Brandon that he knew of a Mr. Broussard from Acadia Parish who sold "hoodoos" in Crowley for getting a mate. The same informant identified a Mr. Girouerd of Gueydan who had sold old man Le Magne a charm for $5 to assist him in finding lost treasure. And

Girouerd, Saltzman cited, although dead now, never charged money for his services and was always glad to deal cards to help others find treasure. Mrs. Courtney La Bauve of Abbeville recounted how a friend of the family once believed his wife was ill due to a gris-gris after the couple had discovered litttle red bags inside their mattress, in the corners of the yard, behind beds and elsewhere. Doctors had not been able to help the wife's condition, and another gris-gris had to be obtained to counteract the first gris-gris. According to the family the "cure" worked.

Some informants asked about hoodoo in Vermilion Parish often had not heard the term—instead they simply identified any such activity as conjo or conjoing. Such is the case with an eighty-six-year-old-informant, Mrs. A. S. Touchet, who was born and raised and who spent some sixty-five years in the Meaux community. After thinking for a while on the matter Mrs. Touchet (in 1990) was able to rattle off the name of three conjo practitioners in her Meaux community: a neighbor, Mrs. Aube; her brother-in-law's mother; and Mrs. Comeaux, her daughter's mother-in-law—all were known to use conjos. Though Mrs. Touchet did not know how they came by their knowledge, she knew the practitioners to be believers in spells and conjo bags. Despite the mystery that surrounds the conjo and its practitioner, the informant had feared only one of the parties, a Mrs. Comeaux, who supposedly could use her skills for harm.

Elizabeth Brandon' s research on superstitions in Vermilion Parish. suggests that the area's isolation, coupled with the black Haitian influence imported with slavery "help explain the persistence of such beliefs where horror superstitions outweigh less frightening beliefs and the expression of faith and trust in religious symbols and figures."[63]

Dolls, Graveyards, Shapeless Horsemen:
Lafayette Parish Hoodoo Accounts

These belief systems are not restricted to Vermilion Parish. In the early 1970s an informant learned that her sister, a native of Vermilion Parish, a resident of Youngsville (in nearby Lafayette Parish), and a devout Protestant had sought out the services of a hoodoo practitioner and had fashioned a hoodoo doll resembling her son-in-law to drive the boy away from her daughter. The woman's son-in-law, it is reported, was so frightened at discovering the doll under his bed that he abandoned his wife and never returned to their home—a trailer parked in his mother-in-law's backyard.

Mr. Bourque of Lafayette recalled his father recounting stories about hoodoo. In a 1969 interview, Mr. Bourque told of a young man who had mistreated his girlfriend. To avenge the wrong, the girl journeyed to a local cemetery and removed a clump of clay from the graveyard and the next day placed a bit of the clay in her boyfriend's coffee—he died. Mr. Bourque also recalled his father's contention that some local hoodoo believers always make it a point to return home straightaway after a funeral; to do otherwise means death in one year and one day to the poor soul who crosses the hoodoo belief.

One interesting account involved an acquaintance of Mr. Bourque's father who would not believe stories that a local stray cat was a man-eater. A short time after declaring his disbelief, the man was found by neighbors clawed to death and local hoodoos interpreted his death as a "spell" cast on the unbeliever. Still another of Bourque's stories advises anyone who comes upon money located in a tree not to say damn when they spy the money for "cuss" words will hoodoo the money and the prize will disappear in an instant—even as you look upon the money and even if you are touching the treasure. Finally, Mr. Bourque was asked for his thoughts on the difficulty researchers encounter in trying to collect information on hoodoo in the area. The informant could only conjecture that local folk's reluctance to discuss such matters could be based on the notion that anyone who discloses the identity of a hoodoo dies—a view his father had told him about as a boy.[64]

William Henry, a black teenager from Scott and his uncle Pierre were firm believers in hoodoo. William had heard stories of a local man who one day was riding horseback when a spirit jumped on the horse and caused the animal to gallop out of control. William was convinced that the story was true because one evening he was walking alone and felt a presence, a spirit next to him. From that day on, he was convinced of the accuracy of the hoodoo stories told in the Scott area. William's uncle had also "seen" a hoodoo spirit. Returning on foot from a social meeting, he and his wife decided to cut across a wooded area despite admonitions from old-timers not to do so. Suddenly the couple noticed a horse in the distance. The animal seemed to be riderless, but on closer observation was ridden by a shapeless form, a spirit. The couple approached the apparition a number of times for a closer look, and each time they did, the horse distanced himself from them. Up ahead was a narrow bridge that stood over a small body of water. The horse and his occupant would have to cross it, and then Pierre would be able to confirm his observation. The horse and its rider never crossed the bridge; they vanished into thin air.

An Acadia Parish Suicide

A college student suffering from depression and released from a Lafayette
psychiatric facility in 1982 reported that after her hospital discharge she had
sought out an Acadia Parish practitioner who had cast a spell over her and
removed "evil spirits" and contaminated tissue from her body. She insisted
that for the first time in months she was not depressed and could enjoy life.
This nineteen-year-old woman committed suicide some weeks after reporting
this incident.

Iberia and St. Martin Parishes: Cradles of Hoodoo

A publications assistant at the Center for Louisiana Studies recalls Fr.
Brown in the 1970s admonishing his Breaux Bridge parishioners at St.
Bernard Catholic Church not to continue Voodoo activities while practicing
the faith. Another informant suggests that these hoodoo practices were
observed in many of the Cajun parishes of Southwest Louisiana.

These beliefs and practices persist. On March 22, 1990, the Iberia
Parish Sheriff's Office, knowing of my interest, acknowledged that it and the
St. Martin Parish Sheriff's Office deal with cases of hexing by black candles
and Voodoo dolls on a monthly basis. The likenesses of prominent people
in the area are placed on Voodoo dolls and are discovered by frightened
parties who bring in the evidence to the police. The police then inform the
"hoodooed" of the curse.

In 1990 informants can still identify dozens of Voodoo practitioners
in the area. Contemporary informants have detailed the names and addresses
of active practitioners in Vermilion, Acadia, and St. Martin parishes.

An Iberia Parish "expert" who has practiced the rites provided the following
accounts of Hoodoo activity in the area.

Interesting accounts are still told of past and present Voodoo mistresses
in the area. Mama Claude, for example, in the 1940s operated a bar on
Pershing Street in New Iberia. Known by locals as a cook, she was also
known to be a hoodoo practitioner. Her bar featured a "red light" welcoming
the patron and curtains in doorways to protect against the spirits. Born
Ollie Kennedy, Mama Claude was a regal looking woman in her eighties
when the informant first interviewed her. Claiming to have done many
"favors" for people in her lifetime, Mama Claude was a yellow-skinned lady
who owned a drawer full of jewelry that she claimed was donated by

satisfied "clients." At the time of her death, mourners gathered from around the country. Mama's casket was displayed in the rear section of her Pershing Street bar. Her body was covered with a purple shroud and her hands held red rosary beads in the traditional Southwest Lousiaina hoodoo manner of warding away spirits. Not buried for three days, Mama's family and friends explained that the soul had a "double" and that three days were needed to assure that the double had achieved its destination—any premature tampering with the soul could result in bad luck or possession for surviving friends and family.

This incident is not isolated. In the 1960s and 70s, the same informant reports attending funerals in rural Iberia and St. Mary parishes and viewing bodies with a shroud covering the face and red beads in the decedent's hands. Mourners at these funerals were often seen tapping the body's shoulder and dropping notes into the open casket, and an examination of the notes found that the slips of paper carried final messages to the deceased attesting to the mourners' friendship and favors—all to assure that the deceased spirit would not meddle in the life of the mourner.

Mother Decuir was another well-known South Louisiana hoodoo practitioner. It is reported that elected officials in Iberia and St. Martin parishes often turned to her to predict election results. With a close relationship to the large black community in these areas, Mother was understandably accurate in many of her political predictions. That politicians trusted her "divining" may indicate the superstitious nature of some people in the rural areas of Louisiana. Mother Decuir believed strongly in the efficacy of hoodoo practices. And although she was often unable to explain the origins of such beliefs, she nonetheless followed the traditional ways passed down to her. An altar in the house, Mother Decuir burned candles, spoke in unknown tongues, had mild trances, treated maladies, and claimed to make her house move with her "powers"—her house was located a few blocks away from a railroad track.

Marie Pitre of Breaux Bridge thought herself a Voodoo witch and informants found her neighbors to be afraid of her. A supposed practitioner, Pitre was a fierce looking black woman who made her living as a midwife, and according to her neighbors at "doing bad things." Utilizing traditional hoodoo practices, Pitre lived in a house painted blue with a pigpen to match—blue was believed to keep away the spitits.

Despite the presence of a body of practitioners, it does not apppear that any organized Voodoo activity exists in Southwest Louisiana. Instead locals "hear" about hoodoo practitioners, and believers (many of them desperate and without hope) simply seek them out for assistance in dealing with illnesses, relationships, and finances.

Oral transmission also plays a role in maintaining practices; hoodoo ways in these parts are orally handed down and reflect a combination of Catholic, Haitian, and African influences. The peculiar nature of what is termed "hoodoo" by the locals is seen by some as an isolated area's adaptive response to a hostile environment.[65]   Without much formal religious education owing to the shortage of priests in the heavily Catholic diocese once deemed the "Wet Grave" by missionaries (due to the area's tropical climate and preponderance of tropical illnesses), and with few doctors, paved roads, hospitals or contact with the outside world until well into the 1930s, the area's inhabitants out of necessity developed a "do-it-yourself" religion to explain life's complexities and to control some of life's experiences seemingly out of man's day-to-day control.

Reflecting this orally transmitted and do-it-yourself quality to faith-life, in the prairies of Southwest Louisiana hoodoo beliefs differ from area to area, and from person to person. Still the basic belief is there, and is handed down from generation to generation.

Some find it amazing that these beliefs survive. An informant some five years ago was surprised when unable to convince a school girl on an educational field trip to enter her historic home's grounds because the girl claimed to have been taught that the abundance of old, draping oak trees was too powerful and menacing a force to cross. This was a unique case, but a series of unique cases appear when field studies are conducted. For example, a few years ago an elderly man approached an authority on hoodoo in New Iberia after claiming to have witnessed a headless man. According to area hoodoo belief, each person possesses a seen and an unseen head, and the frightened gentleman expected the spirit of the headless man to do him some harm.   He remained indoors until the "authority" performed "uncrossing" rites and freed him of any spirit influence.

F.B.I. Seeks Services of Hoodoo Practitioner

In 1971 federal authorities, the state attorney general, and the St. Mary Parish district attorney discussed a complaint of alleged civil rights violation lodged by the Earl Kirt, Sr., family of St. Mary Parish. Mr. Kirt claimed that his neighbor had "hoodooed" the Kirt yard by placing a mound of oyster shells with a cross in its center in his family's backyard. Since the devil now possessed the grass, the Kirt family refused to mow the lawn and unleash these spirits; the yard became an unmanicured mess; the neighbors complained; and the Kirts filed a civil rights action against the neighbor's hoodoo activity. Stumped, local, state, and federal officials approached the New Iberia hoodoo authority hoping that she could conjure a counteragent and satisfy the family's demands for freedom from the evil hand of hoodoo. The "exorcism" was reportedly successful, and the Kirt family dropped its suit.

In part, the "uncrossing" may have been fruitful because the "practitioner" made use of those hoodoo elements held in common by various believers in the rural areas of the state. Realizing the psychologial dimension to the hoodoo experience, the practitioner's ceremony incorporated what the area's believers perceive as essential to removing hexes— readings from the Bible, the use of "uncrossing" powder—Van Van incense packaged in Chicago and sold in local stores, talking in an unknown tongue—in the Kirt case the "practitioner" spoke and incanted in Spanish— a language unknown to the family, and self-confidence on the Other staple hoodoo items are well known in the area. Candles and "Saint Cards" are used in many of the hoodoo ceremonies. It seems that power is sought out by believers from any commonsense source. Catholic priests find it difficult to believe that some people actually tug at them in order to obtain a measure of their power as men of God. Eggshells and chicken bones are accepted agents for casting spells on others. High John the Conq(uer) root is sold in groceries and pharmacies and is used to ward off ghosts, evil spirits, and to usher in good luck especially in gambling. Potions are used to attract love, end a relationship, and deal with many of life's unpleasantries. The snake, a Ewe Vodu staple, and the Louisiana Voodoo oracle, is only used in powder or dried skin form in the rural areas, but is believed to give power over others. Feathers waved in one's face can be used to bring on a headache, a stomach ache, good luck or possibly even death. Notice how the Animist belief that the "charm" is neutral—it can be used for good or for bad—is still alive in many of these local hoodoo practices. Most feared by believers is the spell that combines a black candle, the 3 of Spades, and the Voodoo doll since this spell cannot be uncrossed except by the person who designed it.[66]

Science's Explanations

Folklorists and others have discovered evidence of Voodoo beliefs not only in Louisiana but in various parts of the United States as well as in various parts of the world. Even scientists have examined Voodoo. Harvard physiologist, Walter Cannon, published a classic study, "Voodoo Death," in

1942 in which he asserted that Voodoo could kill. He explained, "'The force that really killed...was the fatal power of the imagination working through unmitigated terror." In other words, the victim "[believed] in the power of the medicine man so strongly he scared himself to death."[67] Not restricted to any one social or economic group, the belief system seems related to man's need for control in a world filled with uncertainty and partial knowledge. Cases of Voodoo hexes and of resulting death are reported from time to time around the country. Dr. Curt Richter of Johns Hopkins Hospital proposes that some Voodoo fatalities are due to "vagal deaths"—the hexed person, like the experimental rat that is placed in a water container, often struggles for a few minutes and then stops all attempts to save itself—it succumbs to despair in the face of what it perceives is a hopeless, helpless situation.[68]

The anthropologist, Marvin Harris, in 1984 made a number of interesting points about Voodoo death around the world. First of all, Harris points out that Voodoo death is no longer dismissed as primitive superstition. "Confronted by many cases in which there seemed to be no medical reasons for death, anthropologists and psychiatrists came to accept Voodoo death as a pathology...Of course, it is the victim's mental state that makes sorcery effective, not bone-pointing or effigy burning." Harris also explains modern theories that account for Voodoo death. One emphasizes "'the power of suggestion' for if faith can heal, despair can kill." Another theory is physiological: " Death is caused by extreme fright and despair which disrupt the sympathetic nervous system and paralyzes vital body functions." A simpler theory holds that the victim's family members block off life-support systems as in Australia's Arnhem Land when after a hexing, "they gather close to the sick-bed, wailing and chanting songs heralding the imminent return of the victim's soul to the sacred well from whence it came. They bring a funeral cloth and lay it down near the doomed loved one. It is not long before the person becomes convinced that this is the

time to die. Appetite fails and the victim makes little or no effort to eat or drink. The assembled relatives often do their part by keeping water cans beyond reach, despite temperatures well above one hundred degrees in the shade."[69]

Some folklorists believe that modern Americans carry good luck charms, knock on wood, cross their fingers—all behaviors that have ancient origins and that reflect a widespread unofficial religious attitude that permits behavior ranging from simple prayers, veneration of religous items, faith promoting items to elaborate folk religions such as the Voodoo practiced in New Orleans.[70]

A Complex Subject

Various historical and cultural developments interacted in a very complex manner to create what is now regarded Louisiana Voodoo. Largely based on West African Animism and influenced by European superstition, Catholicism, and the areas's unique geography, history and culture, Louisiana Voodoo and rural hoodoo are two fascinating dimensions to a rather widespread world experience with similar belief systems.

Further investigation is needed and is likely to shed more light on the Voodoo experience in various parts of the Pelican State and on the forces that make it possible for this phenomenon to persist. Readers should keep in mind that Voodoo activities are secretive and that informants often confide only those select details they care to share. The true face of Voodoo is indeed heavily veiled.

A partial picture at best, this introduction is intended to acclimate the reader to the historical context from which sprung Louisiana Voodoo. The following newspaper accounts and interviews provide a rich feel for the fact and lore of Louisiana Voodoo practices past and present. These sample articles will reveal the many faces of Voodoo—the real and the imagined, the old views and the new ones.

Notes

[1] *Random House Unabridged Dictionary.*

[2] George Simpson, *Black Religions in the New World* (New York, 1978), pp. 60-68.

[3] *Ibid.*

[4] Niles Puckett, *Folk-Beliefs of the Southern Negro,* (Chapel Hill, 1926), pp. 160-67.

[5] Simpson, *Black Religions,* pp. 51-70.

[6] Alfred Metraux, *Voodoo in Haiti* (New York, 1957), pp. 30-38.

[7] *Ibid.*

[8] Metraux,*Voodoo in Haiti,* pp. 30-39.

[9] *Ibid.*

[10] Simpson, *Black Religions,* pp. 60-80.

[11] *Ibid.*

[12] Puckett, *Folk Beliefs,* p. 167.

[13] Robert Tallant, *Voodoo in New Orleans* (New Orleans, 1983), pp. 50-110; see also Rhodes, "Marie Laveau," *Ms.* Magazine, XI (1983), 28-31.

[14] Carl Brasseaux, "French Louisiana's Senegambian Legacy," *Senegal Narrative Paintings* (Lafayette, La., 1986), pp. 56-58; Gwen Hall, *Social Control in Slave Plantation Societies* (Baltimore, 1971) p. 221.

[15] Tom Schick, *Healing and Race in the South Carolina Low Country* (Madison, Wis., 1986), p. 107.

[16] Puckett, *Folk Beliefs,* p. 167.

[17] *Ibid.*

[18] *Ibid.*

[19] George P. Rawick, *The American Slave* (Westport, Ct., 1972), pp. 7-40; Hall, *Social Control,* p. 221.

[20] Metraux, *Voodoo in Haiti,* pp. 30-38; Hall, *Social Control,* p. 220.

[21] John W. Blassingame, *The Slave Community,* (London, 1979), p. 41.

[22] *Ibid,* p. 32

[23] *Ibid,* p. 108

[24] Carl A. Brasseaux, "The Administration of Slave Regulations in French Louisiana," *Louisiana History* (1980), 115-42.

[25] Joe Gray Taylor, *Negro Slavery in Louisiana,* (New York, 1963), p. 34; Blassingame, *The Slave Community,* p. 41; Rawick, *From Sundown to Sunup* (Westport Ct., 1972), pp. 39-40.

[26] Rawick, *From Sundown to Sunup,* pp. 39-40; Taylor, *Negro Slavery in Louisiana,* p. 40.

[27] Taylor, *Negro Slavery in Louisiana,* p. 34.

[28] *Ibid,* p. 130.

[29] Puckett, *Folk Beliefs,* pp. 167-82.

[30] Blassingame, *The Slave Community,* pp. 1, 124-82.

[31] Rawick, *From Sundown to Sunup,* pp. 7-40.

[32] Puckett, *Folk Beliefs,* p. 167

[33] *Ibid;* Mary A. Owen, "Among the Voodoos," *International Folk Lore Congress* (1891), 230; Seymour, "A Voudou Story," New Orleans *Times Picayune,* July 3, 1892.

[34] H. C. Castellanos, *New Orleans As It Was* (New Orleans, 1895), pp. 99-100; Puckett, *Folk Beliefs,* p. 141.

[35] Puckett, *Folk Beliefs,* pp. 181-85.

[36] *Ibid.*

[37] Rhodes, "Marie Laveau," *Ms.* Magazine, XI (1983), 28-31; Martinez, *Laveau: Voodoo Queen, and Folktales Along the Mississippi* (New Orleans, 1956), pp. 20-60.

[38] *Historical Sketch Book* (New York, 1885), p. 229.

[39] Touissant Desossiers, *Haitian Voodoo* (New York, 1970), pp 35-39.

[40] Tallant, *Voodoo in New Orleans,* pp. 100-30..

[41] Rhodes, "Marie Laveau," p. 41.

[42] Tallant, *Voodoo in Louisiana,* p. 11.

[43] Rhodes, "Marie Laveau," 28-31.

[44] *Ibid.*

[45] *Ibid.*

[46] Tallant, *Voodoo in New Orleans*, pp. 110-30; Rhodes, "Marie Laveau," 28-31.

[47] *Historical Sketch Book*, p. 229.

[48] Castellanos, *New Orleans As It Was*, pp. 99-100.

[49] Rhodes, "Marie Laveau," 28.

[50] Puckett, *Folk Beliefs*, p. 14.

[51] Harold Corlander, *A Treasury of Afro-American Folklore*, (New York, 1976), p. 50.

[52] Schick, *Healing and Race in the South Carolina Low Country*, p. 107.

[53] Puckett, *Folk Beliefs*, p. 194.

[54] *Ibid*, pp. 191-92.

[55] *Historical Sketch Book*, pp. 229-31.

[56] Tallant, *Voodoo in New Orleans*, p. 169.

[57] *Ibid*, pp. 180-83.

[58] Rhodes, "Marie Laveau," 28-31; Tallant, *Voodoo in New Orleans*, p. 162.

[59] Elizabeth Brandon, "Superstitions in Vermilion Parish," *The Golden Log*, (1962), 110-17.

[60] Rickels, "The Folklore of Sacraments and Sacramentals in South Louisiana," pp. 27-44.

[61] David Amelquist, "Hoodoo and Voodoo Today," Collection #168, Rickel's Folklore Collection, University of Southwestern Louisiana.

[62] Brandon, "Superstitions," pp. 110-17.

[63] *Ibid*, p. 117.

[64] Amelquist Collection: housed in Rickels Folklore Files, University of Southwestern Louisiana.

[65] Brandon, "Superstitions," p. 111.

[66] Confidential Interview with a Hoodoo practitioner, notes in University of Southwestern Louisiana Archives.

[67] Douglas Colligan, "Extreme Psychic Trauma is the Power Behind Voodoo Death," *Science Digest*, LXXX (1976), 44-48.

[68] "Voodoo Kills by Despair," *Science Newsletter*, LXVII (1965), 284.

[69] Marvin Harris, "Voodoo Death," *Psychology Today*, XVIII (1984), 16-17.

[70] Jan Brunvand, *The Study of American Folklore*, (New York: 1986), pp. 15-17.

Voodoo
Past and Present

Voodoo Conjures Up Big Business in New Orleans
by Steve Brooks for the New Orleans *Times-Picayune*, August 16, 1988.

Voodoo.

Speak the word aloud and notice what happens to your spine.

Few words in the language carry as much fascination or evoke such fiercely opposing responses.

Depending on whom you talk to, it's a venerable religion, a sinister cult, entertainment, a unique slice of New Orleans history, powerful magic or bunkum.

And Voodoo is something more: a business, one of New Orleans' oldest.

"Voodoo has always been commercial," said Kaia Livers, an actress who manages the New Orleans Historic Voodoo Museum and occasionally dances with an 8-foot python out on the bayou.

Practitioners say commercial voodoo is the public face of a religion practiced underground here since the early 1800s.

While slaves met secretly to hold voodoo gatherings that were banned by law, a free man of color named Dr. John advertised himself as a voodoo and charged Creoles to make talismans and place and lift curses.

Robert Tallant's 1946 book *Voodoo in New Orleans* said the business was lucrative enough for Dr. John to build a house on Bayou Road, own slaves, drive a fine carriage and bury $150,000 in his yard. He didn't trust banks.

He was soon overshadowed by Voodoo queen Marie Laveau—New Orleans' first prominent businesswoman—who charged curious whites $10 a head for admittance to mass rituals on the lakefront. She ran a thriving consulting business, selling potions and gris-gris bags to the wealthy.

A public-private split still characterizes voodoo, those in the business world said.

"What you see here (at the museum) is what has been allowed to be seen, " Livers said. "They (voodoo practitioners) won't release their true secrets."

There's good reason for secrecy, said Voodoo Museum founder Charles Gandolfo: "If you open up a ritual, there's a big rush. Police start to pay attention."

Gandolfo cited a recent ritual that had been scheduled at a family cemetery in a St. James Parish cane field.

When the sheriff's office got wind of the plans—in part because Gandolfo was leading ABC's "Good Morning America" crew out to film it—police turned up to ask attendees for identification and participants melted away into the cane.

Because most followers keep quiet, no one knows how many there are here.

"To get a precise estimate would require an intensive-type survey in which you talked long enough to make friends with somebody," said Tulane University anthropology professor Munro Edmonson.

In other American cities with large West Indian populations, voodoo traditions are strong. A 1983 survey of Hispanics in New York by Roman Catholic priests estimated that 70,000 patronized voodoo or Santeria (a Hispanic relative of voodoo) shops and 25,000 believed in food or animal sacrifices.

Estimates range from 5 to 15 percent on how much of the Orleans Parish population is involved in some form of voodoo.

While the faces of commercial Voodoo in New Orleans are as diverse as the people who practice it, voodoo businesses can be classified in three groups:

Tourist Businesses. The biggest voodoo businesses in the area are probably the four shops in the French Quarter that offer voodoo to visitors.

There, one finds a mixture of voodoo and merchandising a world away from the tradition of the elderly women with the "mother wit" down the street.

For example, Chicken Man, a French Quarter fixture who recently opened Chicken Man's House of Voodoo on Bourbon Street, sells candles and other items with his version of a Good Housekeeping seal affixed; "Blessed by Chicken Man."

Livers tells of a client with a failing $100,000 business in Baltimore who called and offered her $1,000 to do a ritual for him. She said she told him his business would be better off if he held on to the money.

Few of the shops will disclose their revenues. Chicken Man estimated he averages $200 to $300 a day.

The Voodoo Museum charges tour groups up to $2,000 for a full-tilt ritual out in the swamps, including a snake dance, the ceremony most demanded by tourists.

Ava Kay Jones, the only local voodoo priestess with her own manager, fetches $1,000 as a lecturer and up to $5,000 to perform with her eight piece band, Voodoo Macumba.

"You can count on Ava Jones," said convention planner Patty Habiceh of Conventions à la Carte, "but I don't know how long I'll be able to afford her. Her price keeps going up."

"We hope to make her (Jones) the premier voodoo priestess, " said her agent, Ben Young of Focus 9 Inc. Young said Jones 40 to 50 performances a year are not billed as rituals.

For more modest fees a person can get more modest services. An in house ritual to cure a disease or bring back a lover might run from $50 to $200.

For $10 to $50—generally called a "donation," a visitor can get a mojo or gris gris bag, filled with a mixture of herbs, concocted to fix what ails them, and blessed on the spot by a voodoo doctor. The bag is generally worn inside the clothes or hung in the home.

Chicken Man will bless houses and calculate lottery numbers. He said he does not charge for the numbers, but he won't turn down a $100 check from a grateful client who scored.

Some of the tourism voodoos are benefitting from the Republican National Convention as national TV crews swoop down in search of the real old-time voodoo. Jones has taped a segment for "Good Morning America" and Chicken Man has been filmed by Cable News Network.

Neighborhood Shops. Outside the Quarter few operations identify themselves with voodoo. Those that do cater to a very different clientele.

On one recent stormy night in Marrero, a pickup truck drove up to "Sister Susan" Verdin's shop on Fourth Street. Her neighbor Dudley hopped out and thrust his head between the dangling fringes of beads in the doorway.

"I think you're going to be hearing from my son, Susan," Dudley said. "You gave him some of that money-drawing oil this afternoon. He thought it was pretty funny, but he rubbed it on his hands. Three hours later his wife found an envelope with $86 in it."

Verdin was steeped in the voodoo of rural Louisiana by her god-mother— a God-fearing Baptist who trucked with spirits and cured people by putting a Bible on their heads.

Her shelves are stocked with dolls she made from moss and oils she concocted.

In the rear is a collection of partially melted candles in the shapes of naked men and women. To each candle is tied a scrap of parchment that bears the handwritten name of a person meant to be attracted or repelled.

Neighborhood women gather there some nights for a sort of voodoo coffee klatch, exchanging time-tested recipes such as the following intended to bring money into a house for seven days:

Mix brown sugar, cinnamon and ammonia. Mop your floor with it, starting at the front and ending at the back. Wipe your doorknobs with the ammonia and dump it out the back.

Over on Elysian Fields, JoAnn Jennings, aka voodoo priestess the Rev. Lady Bishop, counsels a steady stream of middle-class black practitioners in the rear of a shotgun house, which she calls the One Way Church of Truth.

Dr. Bishop relies heavily on the Bible in her work of lifting curses from those who are "oppressed, depressed, or just in a mess, " prescribing psalms and prayers to particular saints as well as mojo bags.

She will not disclose the minimum donation for her services, but $100 bills can be seen floating in the chalice of "blessed water" she uses to cleanse them of negative vibrations.

The donations ensure that people follow her prescriptions seriously. "If you don't make people make a sacrifice, they won't do what you tell them," Bishop said.

Spiritual Shops and Botanicas. A few avowedly Christian sects such as spiritualist churches have sprung up and incorporate certain voodoo practices.

Felix Figaro, a Puerto Rican immigrant who owns the F&F Botanica Inc. on Broad Street, stocks as complete a collection of plaster saints as can be found at any religious supply shop, along with boxes full of Spanish-language novenas.

He also sells Seven African Powers candles, Black Cat Bone oils and dried plants found in any voodoo shop.

Figaro denies he runs a Voodoo shop. He insists that although he sells black candles with labels that explain how to throw curses, he instructs customers how to fight curses with the candles rather than to place them.

"I don't believe in voodoo," Figaro said, "We don't sell any things bad. I'd feel bad if I was selling something that someone hurt himself with."

Excerpt from *A little of this, a little of that* **by Steve Brooks for the** *Times-Picayune*, **August 16, 1988**

Here on the bayou Voodoo has absorbed elements of Cajun herbology, American Indian practices, and even Pentecostalism.

Thus New Orleans Voodoo "is not a unified set of beliefs or a full cult," said Tulane University anthropology professor Munro Edmonson. "Its more like a series of what the unfriendly would call superstitions detached from one another."

Voodoo includes many elements of mainstream American religion, such as using candles, prayer and incense to appeal to the saints for help.

Not that it's a religion for the squeamish. Voodoo also includes out-of-the-mainstream traditions such as gris-gris and animal sacrifice.

Derived from the French word for gray, gris-gris mixes helpful "white" and harmful "black' magic for purposes such as causing a couple to fall in love or breaking up a couple...

Charles Gandolfo, founder of the Historic New Orleans Voodoo Museum, said the sacrifice of chickens, and goats and the drinking of their blood is sometimes necessary to attract the right spirits.

"People need to see the context," said Gandolfo. "For most rituals you don't have to sacrifice anything, but sometimes you need a stronger power. A lot of spirits want a blood sacrifice."

Behind the Veil of Voodooism in America:
Strange Cult Dealing in Black Magic Brought to American Colonies by Early Slaves, Still Exists Despite Efforts of Police to Stamp Out, **New Orleans** *Times-Picayune*, **October 15, 1930.**
By Hilda Phelps Hammond

'A family in New Orleans awakened not long ago to find a cross of moist salt on the front porch. Neighbors gathered and the newspapers carried headlines concerning this symbol that portended trouble for the inmates of the house, for Voodooism though subdued, still exists in that city.'

If you should wake up tomorrow morning and find a cross of salt upon your front porch, what would you do?

If you lived in Iowa or Michigan or even in Pennsylvania you would probably sweep it away and call it a neighbor's prank. But if you lived in Louisiana you might act quite differently—for a cross of salt, in the language of voodooism, means trouble!

That is why Mr. and Mrs. Joseph Gauthier of New Orleans thought twice before sweeping away the cross of salt that they found on their porch a few months ago and that is why the neighbors flocked to the Gauthier home to examine it and the newspapers carried headlines about it. For voodooism is not dead in New Orleans. It has been trampled upon by the police, it has been scoffed at by the intelligent element of the city, it has dwindled, withered, lost many of its followers—but it still lives!

Three feet by two the cross spread itself, and the caked mass indicated some one had placed the salt there in a thoroughly dampened condition. There were neighbors who insisted that they had heard strange noises in the early morning hours: there were others who spoke of seeing a dark form glide past the house: there were some who had heard nothing but the baying of hunting dogs. But on one thing all agreed: a cross of salt does not mean death. A coffin with a name written upon it with pencil dipped in vinegar would mean that, or an acorn stuffed with hair and bearing four holes in its side, but a cross of salt means only trouble.

The neighbors stood and gossiped. Some recommended throwing finely chopped basil leaves over the cross to destroy the "gris-gris": some staked their all on a frizzly chicken, most potent of spell-breakers, but gradually they began to speak of other things and to recall the tales told by their grandmothers and great-grandmothers of the days when voodism was at its zenith in Louisiana.

Tales of the swamps where the voodoo worshippers gathered on St. John's Eve to dance in wild ecstasy; tales of Dr. John, whose house on Bayou road was sought by those who wished to gain fortune or love or domination over the mind of a hard master: tales of Marie Laveau, the greatest queen that the cult ever bowed to, and of her successor Malvina Latour, calm, deliberate and powerful names almost forgotten, but names that once struck terror into the hearts of thousands. Names whose owners have gone forever, but which still remind one from time to time of that short, strange chapter in Louisiana history.

What is voodooism?

Voodism was evidently introduced into Louisiana by the slaves shipped over from the African coast. Great, rough creatures they were, uncivilized and untamed, who well deserved the name "brutes" that was given to them because of their brute force. Captured in battle on the African coast by cannibal chiefs, these unfortunates were sold to the owners of slave ships and brought to the United States. Some of them died on the journey, some of them threw themselves overboard in despair, but hundreds of them landed in Louisiana and were put to work on the slave farms in the swamps. They were soon taught to use the ax, to clear the ground, to build houses, and before long New Orleans had its organized slave labor.

Ignorant and unhappy, with only the words of their tribe upon their lips, these slaves brought with them from their African homes the superstitions and beliefs which had been instilled into their savage minds. The god Voodoo was their idol—antagonist of the African god Zombi—and to him they still went in adoration. Terrible in his wrath was this Voodoo, able to wreak vengeance upon those who defied him and to aid those who appeased him. His earthly form was believed to be that of a living writhing snake.

Intensely emotional, the Negroes gave themselves to the worship of Voodoo and met in remote spots in the marshes to entreat this spirit to give them power over their enemies. Secret indeed were these meetings and those who participated in them swore an oath never to reveal what went on at these conclaves—an oath sealed by smearing the lips at one part of the ceremony with the blood of a slaughtered animal. And such a ceremony it was!

Dore might well have drawn the picture.

The whirling, beseeching forms, the imperious king and queen—distinguished from the others by blue cords around their waists—who conducted the ceremonies, the hissing snake upon the altar, the Negroes with red handkerchiefs about their loins. The chanting, humming, dancing—louder, faster, more furious until the whole place was a mass of bodies turning, twisting, falling prostrate at last! And at all times the voices—pleading, begging, imploring—and the sound of feet in weird unison marking time as they sang. In the early days of voodooism those songs were tribal in their language and the swamps would resound to the barbaric, "Eh, eh, Bomba, hone, hone."

Later the Creole patois crept into the songs—crept into them just as the white blood crept slowly into the veins of the Africans and made mulattoes, quadroons, and octaroons of this race. And then the "Catabaflo tay" changed itself into the rhythmic "Dansez Calinda Badoum! Badoum!" For the eighteenth century saw voodooism introduced into to the colony, but it was in the nineteenth century that this cult reached its pinnacle of notoriety.

Dr. John was probably the first voodoo king whose reputation was city-wide, and the stories have it that not only did the Negroes seek his counsel, but that carriages would drive up to his house on Bayou road and out of them would step heavily veiled ladies who wished their identity concealed but who paid heavily for the charms of this fellow whose tattooed face and frilled shirt front were known far and wide. Lizards, toads, littles phials of strange compounds, pebbles, and shells with which he read the future, amulets to protect one from harm—-all these were to be found in that strange house. Hundreds of Negro servants were his followers, and from them he gleaned details of domestic upsets in the households and was well prepared for the trembling, unhappy, ladies who consulted him by the advice of these servants. Little is it to be wondered at that the ladies were astounded at his knowledge of their affairs and believed in his powers.

But of even more interest is Marie Leveau—a personality to be reckoned with. Sometimes the name is found as Laveau, but the old records of the Cathedral show the marriage of Jacques Paris and Marie Laveau, free mulattoes. This woman became the mother of the famous Voodoo queen, but the father was not Jacques Paris, but Christophe Glapion, a mulatto with whom Marie lived immediately after the death of Paris. Of splendid physique and handsome features, the young Marie soon found her way into the households of white families as a hairdresser and many secrets were whispered into her listening ear by demoiselles in love. Love affairs she could quickly cure and ailments produced by gris gris—small bags containing powdered brick, yellow ochre and cayenne pepper—could be speedily overcome by her magic.

Soon she became a leader and queen. True, her kingdom was limited to the swamps of Lake Pontchartrain, were she reigned supreme on St. John's Eve—the 24th of June—and her subjects were of the Negro race but her word was law and she exercised a hold upon the imagination of her race that has seldom been equaled.

It is told that when a hurricane passed over the city in the later years of her life, she was living in a shanty on the shores of Lake Pontchartrain. The wind rocked her cabin back and forth and she was entreated to leave the place and seek shelter in the city. Again and again she refused help, but finally consented to leave her abode, and no sooner was she safely away than the cabin disappeared into the water. The superstitious Negroes declared that at the moment that Marie Laveau was safe, the storm abated. In an article by G. William Nott it was stated that "an old gentleman who remembers Laveau from his childhood days would tell how she was held in dread by many of the residents below Canal street, white as well as negro." He describes her as having a "Voltarian " look, penetrating and taking in everything at a glance: an attribute quite disconcerting to the children of the neighborhood. They would listen with terror when their black nurses threatened to give them to Marie if they failed to obey.

One has but to look at her picture to feel her force. Dignity, imperiousness, contempt for cowardice, all these things may be found in that mobile, mulatto face. She had a strange beauty that was partly diabolical, partful wistful: who knows what longings filled her tumultuous heart: G. W. Cable was fascinated by the tales told of her and saw her shortly before her death... Three generations of her children were within the faint beckoning of her helpless, waggling wrist and fingers. "She had shrunken away from her skin. It was like a turtle's. Yet withal one could hardly help but see that the face now so withered had once been handsome and commanding. There was still a faint shadow of departed beauty on the forehead, the spark of an old fire in the sunken, glistening eyes and a vestige of the imperiousness in the fine, slightly aquiline nose and even about her silent, woe-begone mouth. Her grandson stood by, an uninteresting quadroon between 40 and 50 years old, but his mother, her daughter, was also present—a most striking and majestic figure. One had only to look at her brilliancies—too untamable and severe to be called charms or graces—to her mother and remember what New Orleans what New Orleans was long years ago, to understand how the name of Marie Laveau should have forced itself inextricably into the traditions of the town and the times. Had this visit been postponed a few months, it would have been too late. Marie Laveau is dead: Malvina Latour Latour is queen.

The queen is dead—long live the queen is a cry also of voodooism. But just how long she lives depends upon herself. Technically she is queen for life, but one can die even while one lives and it seems as though Malvina Latour's name is the last famous one. Certainly a Marie Laveau comes as rarely as a Corday or Cleopatra. But though the queen may not be known, still there are voodoo meetings. It is almost impossible for an outsider to reach such a meeting for secrecy was always thrown about the gatherings and is now a hundredfold greater than ever. Ask any Negro you meet about voodooism and the reply will be a shake of the head and an emphatic denial of any knowledge whatsoever in regard to the ceremony. But win the confidence of one as Lyle Saxon, author of *Fabulous New Orleans*, did, you may be one of the few to witness a modern voodoo ceremony. You may be led to one of the old, uninhabited houses that hang over the banquettes of the old quarter and after you have successfully passed the barriers and safegrounds, and have been admitted to the inner circle you will hear the chanting, the humming: the beating of the drum and will see the writhing bodies, the imploring voices, the beseeching hands that have always belonged to the worshippers of Voodoo. True, there may be modern words to the songs, there may be English on some tongues instead of the Creole patois, but the prayers, the contortions, the coiled snake, the drawing of blood to appease the god, the abom-zoom-zoom of the drum—these will speak of voodooism as it has been for two centuries in New Orleans.

The police are its enemies, but voodooism still exits. Charms are still given to those who trust the gods—feathers from a chicken's breast, hairs from the tail of a white horse, stuffed acorns, pinches of salt to throw over a shoulder.

A Wild Story-1723-The Birth of Voudouism
Appearing in the New Orleans *Daily Picayune* on June, 28, 1874

[A tale used by whites to explain the origins of Voodoo in New Orleans]

There is, on Bayou road, an old house that has defied alike the harms of time and the humid, destructive breeze of our swamps, a breeze before which stone and iron melt away like ice. This building, a sturdy centenarian, has its story, like many a more aristocratic mansion: a story that was universally known and believed half a century ago, but which, like all the old ideas and glories of Louisiana, is fast being forgotten and unheard.

A century and a half ago there lived in the city of New Orleans an old Frenchman, by name, Jean Marie de Castillion. Jean, or "Babillard" as he was rechristened, was an ideal old Frenchman, vain, childish, and garrulous, but the very best of company. His fund of anecdotes was inexhaustible; in these old Jean was always his own hero—victor on the field of battle, in the cabinet or in the drawing room.

Every morning and every evening, Castillon would promenade through the marshy *Places d'Armes,* or along the fish-smelling levee, ogling the *filles de la casette,* or voluptuous sirens from Santo Domingo. Yet, even these could not allure him; and he would wander away from their temptations to the company's warehouses, where he was sure to capture some new listener, a wild, half savage voyageur from Sainte Genevieve or a staid Alsacian from the German coast. Then would he pour forth his stories, until a plea of "business" rescued his unhappy prisoner.

Among the many "coinages of his brain," one never failed to bring down his audience; this was his claim to a Marquisate in the aristocratic province of Berri. Some of the army officers, dangerous pegrès drafted from the prisons of Paris, would jokingly respond to this claim, that old Castillion was more than noble, that he was royal, and bore upon his shoulders, like the kings of France, a blood-red *fleur de lys,* printed there in large characters by the hangman of Arles. At this rough camp joke, Castillon would twist his moustaches, contract his bushy grey eyebrows, and drop his hands upon his sword hilt. He never drew the weapon; his courage was so well established by his stories that this was deemed all that was necessary in such a chevalier Bayard.

With all his nobility and his chateau in Spain, Jean was distressingly poor. He had a house—a rickety, uncertain cabin, provided by the Government—but his cupboard was as bare as that of Mrs. Hubbard, of Mother Goose fame. The neighbors never refused him a meal; for this Castillon always paid most liberally in stories and jokes. When, however, a famine came on and the crops were burnt by the Indians or destroyed by the flood, old Castillon would take his pirogue, meander through the spider web of bayous and lakes that surrounded the city in search of berries, wild fruit, or anything edible he could pick up.

On October 18, 1728 when old Castillon was out on one of these predatory expeditions, occurred one of the greatest storms that ever swept through the Gulf of Mexico. For five days and nights this old Castillon was missing and given up for lost. "The storm," "Indians," "alligators," "carried off by the devil," were the exclamations of his acquaintances, ready to build a two-volume romance on even less foundation than this very natural disappearance.

Just as these stories were growing stale and cold, old Castillon appeared. He had set out a stout, hearty, jovial old gentleman; he returned dirty, haggard, reduced in size and with a strange saturnine scowl upon his usually beaming face. Not a word did he say to the friends who congregated around to greet him, but marched straight to his little hovel in the rue de Conde, pulled up to the plank that served as a draw-bridge to his castle—for in those days every house in the city was on island to itself—and lay hidden from view for a whole week. The only token of his existence was the flame and smoke that curled upwards from his mud chimney, and this flame told some that he was at work in his kitchen, others that the devil was paying him a friendly visit.

When, at the end of a week, Castillon left his hut, he was thinner, more yellow and emaciated than when he had entered it. Instead of promenading on the levee with his supply of yarns for sale, Castillon now frequented a grove of trees that grew just back of the city, about equi-distant from the city walls and the Highlands of the Lepers. Old Marie, Queen of the Voudous, and Buechin, the Indian doctor, were consulted by the curious, but could only explain what everybody knew, that Castillon was bewitched-voudoued.

The following is Castillon's own version of the story.... In his wanderings on the day of his disappearance, Castillon came upon a strange outer grove of trees, known to the Indians as "The Fairies' Grove." Seeing some bright golden fruit that grew luxuriantly upon these tress, Castillon determined to lay in a winters supply of these Hesperian apples, if it should be proved that they were edible. It was not at all an easy task to climb these trees; they were tall, smooth, and almost limbless. Thirty feet from the ground they burst into three branches or limbs, one growing centrally upward, well covered with long wiry leaves; the other horizontally from the side, lithe, thin, and almost leafless.

It was only after superhuman efforts that Castillon reached the fork of the tree. Seating himself there, he greedily devoured one of the fruit that had first attracted his attention. No sooner had he finished it than a strange feeling came over him, the earth seemed to spin around with frightful rapidity, the trees commenced playing leap-frog, and the very sun itself seemed "dancing as on an Easter day." So dizzy did he become, that unable any longer to hold on to he branch, he let go and fell headforemost to the ground.

When Castillon awakened from this shock it was evening; the sun, red with the glow of the coming storm, was just sinking behind the horizon. Yet even a greater change had come over the trees whence he had fallen. Slowly the mighty branches softened into arms, the leaves melted into hair, whilst the scaly bark, dropping from the trunk, exposed to view a face of the most startling beauty. Castillon was almost paralyzed at this sight; he thought that the fall had disordered his brain, or that he was asleep. But no! Everything was distinct, and a pinch assured him that if his mind was asleep his legs certainly were wide enough awake.

Before Castillon had fully recovered from his fright, this new-born "daughter of a race divine" addressed him in soft, melodious music:

"Amidst the hordes of heaven, and the blooming realms of everlasting light," said she, "I once roamed free and happy, until I was commissioned to guard this country, the Garden of Eden, but which now the hand of man has so scourged and ravaged. You know the story well: I did but leave Adam for a second, he could not resist temptation, he fell, gave up immortality for knowledge. He suffered for it, so do I. Within this tree, the tree of knowledge am I forever confined, until I shall be reached by a descendant of Adam. You have eaten of this fruit. To you, now the mysterious language of nature is revealed; the mists that cloud the past and the future are blown away. On you is imposed the task of rescuing us: do you consent?"

So sweet the accent, so fair the face that Castillon whose blood old age had not yet cooled, forgetting alike fear and superstition, sprang from his mossy couch and swore by his life, his honor and his soul that he would rescue them.

After lying there, half stunned, for several days, protected by their Briarean arms from the storm, Castillon recovered sufficiently to come to the city. He daily resorted to these trees, and seated in the branches of one of them, like St. Simon Stylites, seemed to be ever meditating some great problem. His visits to the grove became daily more frequent, and finally he entirely deserted his little hut in the city, and built him an eyrie in the tallest of the trees: never after this did he set foot within the walls.

This, with the sudden change in Castillon's disposition, greatly excited all the gossips of the town. He who had never had a golden portrait of his Majesty, Louis, *le bien-aimé,* suddenly became one of the richest persons in the colony. He was somewhat of a usurer, and never refused the young bloods of the city a loan for a dissipation or a carouse. His money never brought any good, it always corrupted the owner, whispered evil thoughts and wishes, and brought ruin and disgrace on the oldest families of Orleans, Canada, and St. Domingo.

Castillon soon became regarded as a mighty wizard and magician. Thousands resorted to him to solve one love knot more intricate than that of Gordianus, to probe the future, or to get rid of a dangerous rival. In none of these tricks did he ever fail. His prophecies, clear and unequivocal, unlike those of Delphi and Nostrodamus, are still current among the old Creoles and negroes. His miraculous power was always ascribed to his familiars, the trees...

Of course, with all this halo of romance around him Castillon got a monopoly of the supernatural business of New Orleans. A certain essence of his, for one's enemies, which he distilled from the leaves of his trees was fully as popular and effective as aqua tofana.

Castillon was several times suspected and accused of poisoning, but nothing could ever be proved against him. As for his fetishes and pretended magic, the Government was too sensible to interfere; they were part of the religious beliefs of the negroes, and did much to keep quiet a very dangerous class of the population...

On a March morning of 1778, occurred the greatest storm in the history of America, the city of Havana was almost totally destroyed, and it is calculated that two-thirds of the population of Martinique and Dominica were killed. The hurricane swept with unexplained fury around New Orleans and all along the bank of the river.

The next morning a party of soldiers who were sent out to rescue the overflowed farmers on the lake, passing by Castillon's house, they discovered a man swinging by his neck from a branch of a tree. A close investigation showed it was Castillon himself fearfully mangled and torn, and hung like Absalom. Whether he died from suicide, or through an accident, or whether he was himself the victim of those spirit trees, they alone can tell. The [picket] on the city walls said that through the thunder and lightning of the storm he could distinctly hear the cracking and sobbing of the branches of those trees, mingled with the curses and shrieks of old Castillon. Certain is it that, ever after, the trees were dumb and mute, and seemed to have lost all power of speech, and there are some who say that Castillon's life was the last demanded to set these spirits free.

An Excerpt from *"Marie Laveau, Long High Priestess of Voodouism in New Orleans: Some Hitherto Unpublished Stories of Voudou Queen,"* appearing in the magazine section of The New Orleans *Times - Picayune*, Sunday, November 19, 1922, by G. William Nott.

[To some Marie Laveau was the devil incarnate. To others she was a saint.]

Henri Castellanos in his interesting book *New Orleans As It Was*....in his account of the poisoning of a certain Antoine Cambre, convicted of murder wrote: "As the time of his execution was fast approaching, it was on the eve, I believe, Marie Laveau, who had ready access to his cell (it was her custom to visit the condemned to death, bringing them fruits and sweetmeats), approached him, and in her Creole dialect said, "Mon petit, befo you die, tell me what you like to eat and I'll make you a good "lil" dinner." At this proposal, Cambre it is said, mournfully shook his head.

"I'll make you a gumbo file like you ain't never taste in yo' life."

These were prophetic words. Cambre assented and a few hours thereafter was writhing in the agonies of death.

While speaking of prisoners it will not be amiss to relate the story of an octogenarian mammy who says Marie Laveau was not a wicked woman, but much maligned by her enemies, and that what powers she had were used for the good of others, as the following will prove. A certain wealthy young man in New Orleans many years ago had been arrested in connection with a crime, and though his companions were in reality the guilty ones, the blame was laid upon his shoulders.

The grief-stricken father immediately sought Marie Laveau, explained to her the circumstances of the case, and offered her a handsome reward if she would obtain his son's release.

When the day set for the trial came round, the wiley Voodoo after placing three Guinea peppers in her mouth entered the St. Louis Cathedral, knelt at the altar rail, and was seen to remain in this posture for some time. Leaving the church, she gained admittance to the Cabildo, where the trial was to be held, and depositing three of the peppers under the judge's bench, lingered to await developments. After a lengthy deliberation, though the evidence seemed unfavorable to the prisoner, the jury finally made its report, and the judge was heard to pronounce the words "not guilty."

The joy of the anxious father may well be imagined His first act was to find Marie Laveau and as a recompense for her "miraculous intervention, he gave her the deed to a small cottage. The latter, situated in St. Anne Street, between Rampart and Burgundy, remained her home to the time of her death.

As a proof of her charity, an incident is related which though exhibiting the virtue of charity, shows traces of cunning as well. A young man came to her door on one occasion, ragged and destitute, begging for alms. As she herself was short of funds, she could give him nothing, but summoning her nimble wits, she evolved a scheme that promptly bore fruit. Laying the man on a couch in her front room, and covering him with a sheet, she proceeded to light candles which she placed at his head and feet. This done, she stationed herself on the door steps, tin cup in hand, begging the money with which to defray the poor dead man's funeral. The success of the plan was almost instantaneous, she well knew the negroes' love for wakes and cap overflowing with coins, she returned indoors to share the profits with the speedily resurrected "corpse."

Another quaint occurrence in the same house is recounted by an eyewitness.

One of Marie Laveau's proteges had passed away, this time in reality, and the interment was to take place from her "front parlor." Came the hour for the funeral. As soon as the coffin had been borne away, followed by the "queen" and a motley assemblage, three negresses, one with a broom, the others with buckets, and a negro man, rushed out of the house, the former like some ancient furies, and scoured with savage energy the brick "banquette" removing every trace of the mourners' footprints.

The same authority tells of the grotesque saturnalia held on the shores of Lake Pontchartrain. The "voudous" generally chose a moonless night, the intense darkness adding to the impressiveness of the ceremony. A large fire was built, upon which simmered a kettle containing red wine, cinnamon and sundry spices and herbs. After partaking liberally of the steaming "tafia" the participants stripping themselves to the waist would form a ring, and amidst hideous shouts and cries, the signal for the dance was given. An old negro would scrape on a two stringed fiddle covered with snake skin, two young mulattoes would beat upon little drums made of gourds or cow skulls covered with sheepskins, and then the famous "Calinda" would begin. At first a single dancer, then another and another, until finally the whole assemblage took part. The spasmodic jerks and contortions of the dancers keeping time to the primitive tam-tams would increase in intensity with each new addition, until with eyes rolling and mouths foaming, gasping for breath, the frenzied contestants would sink to the floor unconscious...

An old gentleman who remembers Marie Laveau from his childhood days, still tells how she was held in dread by many of the residents...

Whether or not the famous Marie Laveau possessed supernatural powers has long been the subject of discussion among the ignorant.

More enlightened people have discussed her as a crass imposter, though not denying for an instant the prestige she held among her own race.

However, with her death "voudouism" all but disappeared from New Orleans. The little that is practiced today assumes a harmless form; a few chicken bones placed on a door step; a black cross mark on a front board, a bright red powder sprinkled on the banquette; these are the last vestiges of the once dreaded "gris-gris."

In the old St Louis Cemetery on Basin street is a neat brick tomb with the following inscription:

Famille Vve. Paris
Nee Laveau

This is all that remains to recall the former greatness of the all-powerful "Voudou Queen."

The Congo Dance: **An Account Reported in the New Orleans** *Daily Picayune,* **October 18, 1843**

[Whites were curious about the goings on in the Congo Square. A number
of accounts written by white reporters condescendingly reported on the
happenings there in such a way as not to offend any civilized (white)
person's sensibilities]

Many of our readers, we dare say, never saw this favorite dance of our servile population. We never did, till last Sunday afternoon, and now for the benefit of the uninitiated proceed to give our "experience." This ball— this black ball, was a public one, and was held in the capacious yard of a house in the Third Municipality. The company was numerous, and ranged from ebony black to quarteroon yellow. The orchestra was full, and, judging from the satisfaction which it gave, very effective. The leader strummed a long-necked banjo, the head of which was ornamented with a bunch of sooty parti-colored ribbands: another of the musicians beat the jaw bones of an ass with a rusty key: a third had the end of a butter firkin, covered with a tightly drawn sheep skin—a kind of a la petit tambour, on which he kept time with his digits, and a fourth beat most vehemently an old head-less cask that lay on its side, ballasted with iron nails. To these instrumental efforts were given a general vocal chorus.

The dancers were three, a "gem'an negro" and two of the fair sex, color excepted. The latter danced with an air of becoming and commendable modesty; their ambition seemed to be to move their feet rapidly, but still with the least possible visible motion. Their male partners had on a pair of leather knee caps from which were suspended a quantity of metal nails, which made a jingling noise that timed with his music. He indulged in sundry extra things, which apparently ministered to his own self-esteem and to the gratification of the audience. Such is a negro Congo dance in New Orleans.

A Snake Story: reported in the New Orleans *Daily Picayune,* August 13, 1863
[Girl who claims Voodoo snake inhabits her belly gives birth]

A few days ago a colored woman named Susan Williams resided in a house on St. Peter Street. Alleging that she had become the victim of some Voudou incantation, she excited a good deal of sympathy among the dusky daughters of that neighborhood. When asked how she was affected, she persistently declared that she had a snake in her stomach. To dislodge the reptile intruder, she applied to several of the voudou serpent charmers, and obtained from them roots and herbs which she steeped with the infusion of tobacco, and drank the liquid which was thus obtained. The dose was strong and unpleasant, but she was satisfied that it would remove the snake, or at least, give it fits, and with the determination of a true believer, she swallowed the villainous compound. The result, however, was altogether unexpected, save by two or three of the neighbor women who had listened to tales of scandal, and concluded from the first that all was not right. Instead of having the desired effect upon the snake, the voudou drink brought on the labors of maternity, and the patient, to her extreme surprise, became a mother, an event for which she was wholly unprepared. She attributed it all to witchcraft, and expressed her opinion that a child thus brought into this breathing world would never come to good. In the morning the child was dead, whether from inattention or the mother's desire to be revenged upon the serpent does not fully appear clear. Under a certificate from the Coroner, its [the baby's] remains were buried, and the woman, whose condition was extremely low, was removed to the Charity Hospital. The medical resources of that benevolent institution were, however, insufficient for her case, and the day after her admission she too went the way of all the earth. This case is a curious one. If the intentions of the woman were criminal from the first, she certainly met with a speedy and well-merited punishment; and that they were so, is pretty well established by the fact that she persistently denied that she was pregnant, and seemed pleased when informed that her child was dead.

The Condemned; The Decorations of the Altar: appearing in the New Orleans *Daily Picayune*, May 10, 1871
[Another death row cell decorated by Marie Laveau]

Yesterday the reporter visited the condemned cell of Pedro Abriel and Vincent Bayume, appointed to suffer death on the 13th inst. Since Sunday the preparations for their execution have been going steadily on. The prison has been put in a state of complete renovation, and wears an almost holiday appearance. The halls are white, and the casings and iron railings have been newly painted. But this is not the chief feature of interest. This is the condemned cell...

For more than twenty years, whenever a human being has suffered the final penalty in the Parish Prison, an old colored woman has come to their cell and prepared an altar for them. This woman is Marie Laveau, better known as a Priestess of the Voudous. Arriving at the prison yesterday morning, she proceeded at once to prepare an altar for the worship of the men who have been sentenced to expiate the guilt of murder on the scaffold. It consists of a box about three feet square; above this are three pyramidal boxes, rising to a small apex on which is placed a small figure of the Virgin.

The entire altar is draped in white; on each end of the shelving is a vase of green and white artificial flowers, and beside these a smaller vase of pink and white camelias. In the centre rests a prayerbook in Spanish, and framed in gold, leaning against the altar are hung saints pictures around the walls of the cell. Before the altar is drawn a curtain of white muslin, deeply fringed in silver filigree. The aspect of the altar is singularly beautiful and simple.

The men watch these preparations going on with an air of resignation, touching to its sadness. All of their time is spent devoted to religious rites. They seem to entertain little hope of pardon, and are fitting themselves for the soulful change they are soon destined to experience.

It is a sad spectacle, and no heart is so indurated as to contemplate it with indifference.

Voudoued a Boy:
Cruel and Heartless Deed of a New Orleans Witch reported in the New Orleans *Daily Picayune*, May 13, 1893

[No one believed him, do you?]

Ernest Bongee is hoodooed. A terrible potent charm set upon his broad, stalwart shoulders, and his 18 years seems 80 as he moves about with the weight of the dread voudou bearing him down.

Ernest is only 18 and he comes from France where the fascinating absinthe frappe dallies with people's mentality, but even so, he had lifted himself from his home, at 284 East Indiana street, and told his pliable story to that sympathetic detective, Robert Bruce, this morning and asked that gentleman to undertake the peculiar mission of clearing the cobwebby voudou from his brain.

Bongee said he had just arrived in Chicago from New Orleans and was hoodooed. Everything he touched proved a failure. Even life had lost its charms since his introduction to the voudou princess, Mme. Shaffer, residing at 68 Chartres Street, in the Crescent city.

The woman took him by the hand one day, and while delivering a solemn incantation rubbed a popular oil on his back. Since then he has had troubles enough for a dozen men. At one time the voudou woman presented him with an ablebodied hoodoo. He was heir to $18,000 left him by his father. This is where the hoodoo hit him hardest. He signed a paper giving the money to Mme. Shaffer and received the sum of $200 for his signature.

He wanted Detective Bruce to send a man to New Orleans with him to remove the voudou; and secure him some part of the fortune left him.

Bob wasn't up on voudou matters and doubted the tale of the Frenchman. He also doubted the existence of the $18,000 and will not take charge of the case.

Bongee is terribly excited over the bad luck that is following him, and trembles with excitement and fear. He believes the voudou will not be satisfied until her uncanny charm results in his death.

Detective Bruce believes Bongee is crazy and the woman and the money the children of his phantasy.—Chicago Dispatch, July 22

Voodoo by Mail: Business Bared in New Orleans appearing in the New Orleans *Times - Picayune,* May 14, 1927

U. S. Investigating Sale of "Black Cat Bones," "Goofer dust," Etc.

A federal investigation of mail frauds in relation to the distribution of love philters, charms, and voodoo magic has revealed a widespread traffic in fake potions extending from New Jersey to Texas, it was learned Friday when Assistant United States Attorney Edmond E. Talbot summoned several Rampart street merchants, including a druggist, who are said to know "the ins and outs of mail order voodoo." Mr. Talbot declined to indicate the probable action to be taken by the federal prosecutors but admitted that post office inspectors "have unquestioned evidence of mail fraud," though there is some doubt as to placing responsibility for the scheme.

A fictional book, *The Life and Works of Marie Laveau,* which carries the supposed incantations, charms, and methods of the voodoo high priestess, is said to prescribe certain magic substances fo various needs. The cases covered by the voodoo rule of thumb range from that of "The Lady in Trouble with Her Landlord" to "The Lady Whose House Has Been Crossed" and "The Gentleman Whose Love Is Spurned." These things to be disposed of according to voodoo prescriptions, calls for the use of all sorts of things such as "Four Thieves Vinegar," "Eye of Eagle," "Cedar of Lebanon," "Shark's Tooth," "Goofer Dust," "Hotfoot," "Damnation Powder," "Love Powder," "Blood of Hawk," and "Black Cat Bones."

A price list sent with orders to Texas and other states offers a set of black cat bones at $5. "Damnation Powder" is listed at fifty cents a package.

The purpose of the federal authorities was said to be "to break up what is obviously an imposition and fraud upon ignorant persons."

Fish Fry Ends in Voodoo Revel, Police Charge: the New Orleans *Times-Picayune*, April 17, 1925

[Typical of alleged "Voodoo" crimes reported to the police, this piece offers more local color than any substance or proof of Voodoo activity in New Orleans. This article and a number of similar newspaper accounts, though, do testify to the participation of both blacks and whites in these ceremonies.]

Neighbors said they heard "all kinds of noises" coming from 1239 Desire street, the home of Mr. and Mrs. Antoine Vega. So Corporal Roach and Patrolman Blancher and Smith raided. They found Lethe Anderson, 200 pound negress, "raving around."

Twenty negroes, the Vegas and several white men were arrested.

The permit was issued for a "fish fry"but the police say it became a voodoo meeting.

Recorder Leonard fined Vegas $10 or thirty days, his wife $5 or thirty days. The rest of the revelers asked for affidavits, as did the fat high priestess.

Voodoo Yet Rules Faithful Disciples of Dead Sorceress: *The Times-Picayune-New Orleans States*, Sunday, March 7, 1937

[Some 56 years after the death of Marie Laveau, Voodoo faithful continued to practice the queen's unique blend of witchcraft and Christian rituals. This

Marie Laveau, "queen" of the Voodoos in the 19th century New Orleans rites, died many years ago, but her ghost still lingers in the city and inspires a number of her faithful followers to make midnight pilgrimages to her tomb in old St Louis cemetery, No. 2.

Gone forever are the wild orgies in which naked and near-naked adherents of the voodoo faith writhed before Zombi, the snake god. However, the illegal trade in, "gris-gris," strange charms which are said to bring illness or health, food or bad fortune, love or death, still continues.

The philter traffic in New Orleans of today is not limited by race, color or position in society. Under the surface the trade in black magic continues to draw dupes from all classes and races. It is not difficult to ferret out from almost any section of the city persons who make their living by selling black death candles, love powders, and charms of all varieties.

Many of the supernatural formulas compounded by Marie Laveau in her brick-fronted house on St. Ann street near North Rampart street or in her hiding place in the swamps along the banks of Bayou St. John are still used. The ingredients of the modern "gris-gris" are much the same as those used by the tall, imperious mulatto.

Salt, pepper, graveyard dirt, crude soap, hair of many types, coffee grounds, crumbled plaster filched from saint's statues, bits of wire twisted into the shape of crosses, and innumerable other things are used in compounding "gris-gris."

The most usual method of "putting the curse" on an enemy is to scatter "gris-gris' powder on his doorstep. Counter-charms are almost as numerous as charms. One sure proof that Marie Laveau's ghost still rules certain classes of New Orleanians is that numerous doorsteps in certain sections of the city are daily scoured with "anti-gris-gris" and as a result have a pale, straw-colored appearance. Many of them may be seen in the French Quarter.

Those who saw Marie Laveau in the 1840's and 50's, when she was in her prime, described her as tall and having an expression like that of Voltaire. George W. Catlin, famous painter of negroes and Indians, left a portrait of her, portraying her high forehead, her sensual lips, and her penetrating eyes.

During the years when her life and the 19th century were coming to a close, the Voodoo "queen" became emaciated and witchlike. Marie carried forward the tradition of her ancestors in Zombi worship and placed the stamp of her personality upon the thinking of many New Orleanians.

Even at the present time on certain nights her followers creep along the cemetery wall in the darkness and scratch little crosses on the brick and stone front of her tomb. They mumble their petitions and leave again in the darkness.

Her gray ghost haunts the city in which she imperiously ruled the Voodoo rites.

Louisiana Legends of the Loup Garou: Beliefs of Many Races Have Gone Into the Making of the State's Own Folklore Stories appearing in The New Orleans *Times-Picayune*, Sunday, May 20, 1928 By Alex Melancon

[Ever wished you could turn into a bull and defeat your worst enemy or be transformed into a bird and listen in on people's secret conversations and watch their most private moments? Well, be mean, mumble to yourself, curse a little, and the devil is sure to grant your wish. For this is the way one becomes a Louisiana werewolf—a Loup Garou. This excerpt from a rambling newspaper story chronicles the colorful werewolf beliefs of some locals]

In a little blue pirogue that is dragged by a broken mare, Mr. Pegrin drives to his own farming tract beyond the willow trees. Of queer manners is he, with his pepper-gray mustache and his unblinking, staring eyes. It is a matter of record that he once shot a person who called him "old man;" once after midnight he ran several miles chasing a dog that had awakened him. For all that, he is a very good farmer: there are those who pretend to wonder at the amount of work he turns out with the aid of the brown mare; but there are others...

The legendarians nod wisely and wink when you question them. With many a shrewd gesture, they bid you follow him beyond the willows to see what you shall see....What of the black mule hitched beside the mare? Where did it come from? Surely, Mr Pegrin would not so early desert his work, and leave the pair unguided? Where is he now? ...The legendarians, those solemn old fellows, will point to the unblinking, staring eyes of the black mule; you recognize them? No need for further explanation! Mr. Pegrin has transformed himself into a mule.

For once [upon a time] he met the loup-garou. Having acquired the habit of speaking aloud when alone, he was an easy prey, and the loup-garou made him his subject. One dark night he was attacked by an enormous dog. Defending himself quite valiantly, he broke the beast's head with a stick, and when the blood started flowing, the dog changed to his best friend who informed him that he had been held enthralled by some sinister witchery. The friend warned him to keep the matter secret a year and a day, or suffer a similar fate, and Mr. Pegrin attempted to. But the time came when he spoke aloud of the encounter, thinking he was alone, and was overheard. It then being necessary that he spend part of his time as a beast: he made an asset of his mishap by the clever plan of becoming a mule, and greatly facilitated his farm labors.

Could Resume Human Form

Loup-garou (werewolf) is a person transformed into a wolf in shape, and usually in appetite or a person capable of assuming a wolf's form....The story-tellers found a treasure mine in this for weaving marvelous tales to relate over the evening fires. To those primitive persons, the world was an unexplored territory. What lay beyond their own experiences could not be understood—or denied. Their simplicity in knowledge made them accept as facts the idle imagings of whoever happened to speak well.

As the legend passed from mouth to mouth, it was enriched with details, its original form changed to suit the whim of each relater. Different races fashioned their favorite versions, making the parts fit their own needs. Some early religions used these accounts in one form or another. Witches desiring evil power, or the reputation for such, took the superstition unto themselves, elaborating it to a vast ritual. Parents with troublesome children used its tales to scare them off, if not to sleep, at least to silence.

Louisiana Belief Composite

The South Louisiana chroniclers have, as most other people have, a distinct way of treating the superstition. Theirs is a blending of the French and Spanish versions, with traces of others included. The Acadians brought part of the innovations from Canada, while the negroes had influence enough to add a dash of their more primitive conception. The result is a mixture of the very simple and the more complicated with its search for causes.

Thus the animals to which the loup-garou fall victim may be transformed, and are not limited to wolves, as first conceived. Dogs, birds, cows, goats, even inanimate objects, the person under the spell may be changed into. In this manner, the curse becomes rather more of a convenience than a punishment. The victim enjoys the advantage of being able to move quickly and go anywhere unrecognized as a beast or fowl. One jealous husband, it is related, changed himself to a bird to watch his wife when she was alone. Unfortunately he perched upon the back of the chair where she was sewing. Her needle pricked his eye, blinded it, so that afterward he would watch her only half as well.

There is a disadvantage, however. While the person under the spell could, at will, transform himself into whichever beast he desired, he might also be called upon to change at any moment. The time he must spend as a beast is fixed, varying according to his demeanor, and if he has not used the allotted time voluntarily, he may be forced to do so at some unexpected instant. The legendarians tell tales of people in groups missing one member of the party, and seeing a dog or calf in his place. Consider the feelings of the young woman who was in her lover's arms when he turned to a donkey; or put yourself in the place of the man who roped a wild horse only to have it changed to his own mother! Of course, it would be a relief to be transformed into a bull when one's rival in love is getting all the attention, or change to a bird to escape some bore at a party.

Punishment Deserved

All agree that the victim customarily deserves his punishment, for it is through lack of self-control or personal meanness that one may become under the power of the loup-garou. The freeing of a person from the evil power is a test for the rescuer, since he must not under any circumstances speak of the matter before a year and a day have passed. If he cannot so far control himself, he takes the place of the rescued one until someone else frees him.

Cursing is to be avoided, because persons who indulged freely in this vice have been known to be victimized by the devil, chief dispenser of the loup-garou legacies. But worse than that, the legendarians declare, is the perfidious habit of thinking aloud. Persons doing this are in particular danger for it is very easy then to for the devil to inject ideas that they will accept as their own thus feeding to their downfall. One could not tell exactly how this should become effective although there is always the possibility that somebody may overhear them speak of persons they have rescued.

Should one meet the victim while he is a beast, one may save him from the spell by causing him to bleed. Why this curse shoud be necessary is a mystery, although it is conjectured that this part of the superstition comes from Christ's having bled to death to save mortals on earth. Thus blood would again bring about the redemption of a lost one, religion so adding its bit to the legend. The victim, however, would not feel any pain even were he hacked to pieces while a beast. The hard part of the job all falls upon the rescuer who is forced to remain silent. The temptation to mention the matter would, through the devil's influence, become so strong that one might easily go mad under the strain, the story-tellers say.

Some Tales Based on Fact

The loup-garou tales are innumerable, the meetings with the beasts, the perils endured, the variety of things that those under the spell do to cause others to need them, forming a veritable library of black-magic thrillers. Each old man or woman had his or her personal selection. Many attribute to the loup-garou happenings in their own lives easily explained otherwise. Some of the tales they invented, others came from their forebears. Some of the stories are wholly true in all details except that the heroes were real beasts on a rampage instead of human beings who took such form.

Some believe implicity the tales they tell. Having related them so often, they come to carry a touch of truth for their inventors. If challenged, some chroniclers will solemnly swear to their tales, adding that they could not occur nowadays; "but when we were young, strange things were happening to us."

Take Tante Elize and Annette, the gay old maids who are not adverse to an occasional cigarette. For years they have lived alone in an enormous house, and are ever willing to recount their adventure. In their younger days, they say, it was their habit to carry water from the bayou, and place it overnight in tubs. For such water is of a much greater clearness if one permits it to settle.

The inexplicable thing was that each morning the tubs were empty. They filled them every night, in the mornings—the water was gone. Neither could explain how it occurred, they were quite distracted. Then Tante Elize awoke one night to find herself alone in bed, and Annette nowhere in the house. Instantly the thought of the escaping water came to her mind; she went to a window, and looked out. A black and red calf was drinking from the tub. Elize followed it, only to note that it entered the house, and went to her bed. Annette had changed to a calf. Luckily, Elize was able to free her from the dark power.

Final Thoughts

A good rule should work both ways. If a person can be changed to inanimate objects, then the opposite should hold true. In at least one of the tales it does. A loup-garou had been freed near a haystack, and dropped some of his blood upon the hay. Now, the rescuer had kept the matter secret the specified time, but the haystack could not hide the blood for the necessary period. So what was more appropriate than it should be condemned to a life of transformation. A most incomprehensible haystack it became. There was no telling where one might find it. Sometimes it stood in a road, sometimes in a yard, and again in a field. It was said that it changed to a man minus a head whenever it desired to move. Naturally, people were woefully scared by its escapades. The end came when it changed to a gigantic candle burning all through one night, with a fearful brightness. The next morning only the charred center pole remained in a circle of burnt hay.

...A mile away the car is stopped again, there is a flat tire. Must the mechanic leave his beloved out in the night? No! No! He transforms himself into an air pump, and all is well. The car goes on.

Then there is a puncture in the tube, it cannot be repaired. Will the girl stay here, and perhaps catch a cold? Never! The mechanic takes advantage of his power, and turns to an inner tube. He is placed in the casing.

The car halts, the mechanic resumes his human shape, and looks around. Alas! He has aided his rival in bringing the little blonde before a justice of the peace...

A sad thing to reflect upon is the modern disbelief. The loup-garou historians bewail the fact that none will listen to their rales without deriding them. They shake their heads solemnly over these youngsters who question their veracity. Often they must console themselves with the thought that the loup-garou will get them one of these days.

Such are the tales of loup-garou in Louisiana.

"Sudden Death"   an article appearing in the New Orleans
Daily Picayune
[The account's author shared the skepticism of many towards so-called
Voodoo activites and deeds]
—An unknown colored man died suddenly at the corner of Customhouse and Burgundy streets Monday evening. The circumstances created a good deal of excitement, and "voudouism" and "witchery" was loudly talked of by his untutored friends. His disease, however, was probably occasioned by heart disease.

Removal of Curse Ordered : **a news article in the Lafayette, La.** *Daily Advertiser*, **Sunday, February, 11, 1990**

[Voodoo Lives! Well, stereotypes at least do. This Associated Press story
is anachronistic—few away from New Orleans can identify the name of
Marie Laveau, and the judge's actions in this reported proceeding are a
curiosity to most Louisianians]

HAHNVILLE, La. (AP) — Down in south Louisiana, where children grow up hearing about the Voodoo queen Marie Laveau, even judges seem to feel it's better to be safe than sorry where curses are concerned.

District Judge Joel Chaisson, not wanting to take any chances with powers stronger than his, did what any born-and-bred south Louisianian could be expected to do.

Chaisson ordered Ronald P. Edwards, 27 of Des Allemands, to remove a curse as a special condition of probation on charges of simple battery and disturbing the peace.

Edwards, who pleaded guilty to both charges Friday, was arrested the day before after a ruckus at his house. As he was being taken to jail, Edwards warned that he had cast a spell on the arresting deputy sheriff and on the judge who would hear his case. Both would become paralyzed soon, he predicted.

In court, Chaisson asked Edwards if he practiced voodoo. Edwards said it was just a joke.

The judge fined him $200 and put him on a year's probation.

And as a special condition of probation, Edwards was ordered to remove the curse.

Priestess Separates the hoodoo from the voodoo by Wesley Jackson for the New Orleans *Times-Picayune*, May, 23, 1987.

"Too often Americans consider voodoo to be a form of black magic, witchcraft or satanism, based on what they see in movies and on television, much of which is 'hoodoo,' or making fun of Voodoo." The Rev. Lady Bishop

The Rev. Lady Bishop is her name, and Voodoo might be called her game, except that to her, it is no game.

Trained and licensed in the mysterious and often misunderstood practice of voodoo by teachers in Haiti, St. Lucia and the Dominican Republic, Lady Bishop, a native of St. Louis, has decided to cast her lot and spells in New Orleans after brief stays in Atlanta and other cities.

Why New Orleans? "St. Barbara asked me to bring her here," she said "and New Orleans is the voodoo capital of the United States, even though many wrong practices are perpetuated here."

St. Barbara is just one of many Catholic saints to whom Lady Bishop, 37, prays for intercessory help as a priestess of voodoo, which she defines as "an African science tied into the laws of nature, and dealing with spirits and the saints."

"Some of these saintly spirits are unrecognized holy men from West Africa while others are the same saints we pray to in Roman Catholicism," she said.

After 18 years in parochial schools and convents, she still considers herself a Catholic, despite her current vocation.

Lady Bishop, a name adopted by Jo Ann McShane Jennings in her voodoo practices, is a Vietnam war widow who claims to have received the gift of psychic powers and prophecy while in the second grade. She said she has traveled in 46 states, living in 21, and several foreign countries.

She said voodoo is a religion of spirits, deriving its name from vodun, which means "spirits" in some African dialects. She said different spirits are sought out to answer different needs....

"The primary purpose of voodoo is healing with herbs, prayers, rituals and spiritual intercession. Too many people correlate voodoo with pins and needles stuck in dolls to create pain and suffering. That is witchcraft, not voodoo. But it also can be an extension of voodoo in the hands of a person who was evil to begin with."

Lady Bishop said she wants to be known as a "membo, or voodoo priestess, and not as a voodoo queen, as the famed Marie Laveau, "whose memory I love and respect greatly, was mislabeled."

Lady Bishop who proudly displays newspaper articles from various cities proclaiming her to be the nation's premiere voodoo priestess, unabashedly seeks that title. And she is quick to criticize people who claim to be knowledgable about voodoo and its practices.

"When so-called voodoo people here found out that I learned Voodoo from priests and teachers from Haiti and West Africa, they backed away from me...in fear," she said.

She also said, "Biting off heads of chickens is not voodoo, but is a misunderstood, minor form of synthetic magic, bordering on witchcraft."

"Voodoo is not a superstition to those who know about its true meaning," Lady Bishop said. "And because it can be extended by evil ones to become something evil, priests and practitioners in Caribbean, South American and West African countries don't play around with it or regard it as a game."

She said she has a mission of her own in Bani in the Dominican Republic, caring for about 100 orphans.

She plans to open a center on the West Bank in the near future. That church, she said, which is being built on Lapalco Boulevard, near Westminster subdivision in Marrero, will be known as the One-Way Gospel Church of Ministry when it is completed in about 90 days.

While the church is being built, Lady Bishop meets with clients in an incensed-filled Tulane Avenue motel room. She also travels frequently to

Ohio, New York, New Jersey, and Michigan, consulting believers in those areas.

To people other than clients, New Orlean's newest voodoo priestess offers this advice: "The Psalms are very important, almost as much as some of the contents of Mojo bags (gris-gris), herbal potions, or voodoo cemetery ceremonies. For instance, Psalms 9, 67, and 112, prayed together, are helpful in money matters." And her advice on Psalms 5 and 91 is "Don't leave home without them."

Ava Kay Jones

A Visit with the Voodoo Priestess Ava Kay Jones

(From all accounts Ava Kay Jones is one of the 20 most active Voodoo and Yoruba practitioners in the United States. Initiated into Haitian Yoruba rites and working out of New Orleans most of her adult life, Jones is considered one of the preeminent Voodoo personages alive today. I interviewed Jones on March 1, 1990.)

Two days after Mardi Gras, the New Orleans French Quarter was still littered with the refuse left behind by hundreds of thousands of revellers who on Fat Tuesday were intent on one last mad party before Ash Wednesday and the opening of the solemn season of Lent. Turning into Bourbon Street, a row of decaying buildings caught my eye and as I panned up from black top to house top, in the distance was the glitter cast by the sun off of the tops and sides and windows of the new city's mini-skyscrapers.

Now noticing people along the way it seemed that on this day tourists and residents out in the Quarter walked a little more slowly than one expects—their haggard steps a little like the cautious ones of the hungover.

Turning into another narrow Quarter street there were no crowds, no noises, no celebrations—the French Quarter was being forced to make the transition from carnival to reality and even the road crews patching up Toulouse Street seemed barely able to tolerate the changeover as they worked a few minutes, stopped and stood a few minutes, and stared a few minutes into the distance or into the heavens, or into whatever avenue allowed for some temporary escape from the newly returned day-to-day run of things.

The scene contrasted sharply with the fast walking, white-robed figure who appeared and approached 813 Toulouse Street at high noon.

Seeing her, even from a distance, this white clad and turbaned woman, and only this certain-stepped woman who seemed transported from another time and another place could be the priestess Ava Kay Jones, a preeminent figure in American voodoo.

Having previously spoken to her on the phone in hopes of setting up an interview with New Orleans' best known Voodoo figure, Jones' precise and articulate speech had helped destroy any stereotypes I may have had about followers of this ancient African religion.

It came as no surprise then that Jones, my research indicated, had been educated in Catholic schools, had a bachelor's degree in foreign languages, and a law degree from Loyola University of New Orleans.

As soon as I entered Jones' establishment other ideas jumped in my head. The West African music with its upbeat melody that saturated the small shotgun shaped shop comforted me—the music brought me back to my Cajun roots and the joy that my French-speaking extended family created as it joyfully gathered and sang along to similar spirited tunes and spoke and loved everyone in sight—back in those days when French was still the language of choice and Cajun culture ruled the prairies of southern Louisiana.

Soothed by my recollections of simpler days, I waited to interview Ava Kay Jones, and melodically the priestess broke into my daydream as she whispered that all was not ready. The correct incense and candles calling in the appropriate spirits of wisdom needed to be burned and an attitude of prayerfulness was required before Jones could begin the interview. I waited; I thought; this store was like a tiny church with candles on an altar, incense burning, music in the background—but not like the churches I had attended. For one thing, this place was lodged off of Bourbon Street right smack in the middle of a neighborhood known for years—perhaps for hundreds of years—as "the pit of hell," and in this church there were no aisles, but there was a well stocked sales counter full of candles and small saint's statues; here there were no confessionals, but there was a seated, meditating priestess deep in contemplation who seemed an excellent and trained listener; inside 813 Toulouse there were no stained glass windows, but there were gleaming jars containing what appeared to be herbs and roots and spices of all colors, and to the right of me some three feet above my head was no Eucharist but a mop of brown and shining human hair—this was a cathedral like none I'd ever before experienced.

Motioning, Ava Kay Jones invited me to that area of her establishment behind the counter and sat me directly facing her— to my side was an altar of cannisters, jars, potions, and "gris-gris" bags.

What follows is her story—a story that chronicles one Louisiana woman's drive to maintain traditional African religion, culture, music and dance in modern New Orleans.

A Discussion of Selected Topics with Ava Kay Jones Conducted on March 1, 1990

(Ava Kay Jones' responses are presented in summary form)

Q: I've heard many stories about the origins of Voodoo beliefs, but I wonder how an individual comes to believe.

AKJ: Well, I was born into a Thibodaux family that was believing. I was raised a Catholic and I still practice some aspects of the faith . . . But my mother was the biggest influence. She was psychic. During her pregnancy my mother was able to see my

The office of Ava Kay Jones, one of the twenty most active voodoo practitioners in the United States, is located at 813 Toulouse Street, in New Orleans' French Quarter. Jones holds a bachelor's degree and a law degree from Loyola University (New Orleans).

Yoruba and Voodoo Priestess Ava Kay Jones makes a gris-gris bag, consisting of herbs and charms empowered to serve as a talisman for love, happiness, prosperity, peace, protection, and health.

"baby spirit" and she knew that I was special and would have special powers. The spirit appeared to my mother while in Our Lady of Guadalupe Church—the International Shrine of St. Jude— and told her that I would be a "blessed baby." I was even born on Halloween—that was further evidence to the powers I would be privy to. My mother had these powers . . . and my grandfather, but that's another story. My mother had the power of divination. She could see into the future and into the past. Now her (Voodoo) skills were basic since she had no formal training. I recall her using smelly oils and such things. Even my grandmother on my father's side of the family practiced folk Voodoo. I was born into Voodoo.

Q: Your mother had basic skills. So there's formal training involved in Voodoo?

AKJ: Voodoo is a formal religion! Perhaps not here, not now, but Voodoo has temples even in the United States. Mine, for example, is in Atlanta and is very traditional. Anyway, where large numbers of Cubans now reside you see a very organized Voodoo-like religion, Santeria. My training, though, took place in Haiti at the Temple of the Cloak of St. Peter. There I was initiated into the rites of Vodun and am able to practice various levels of Vodun ritual based on my advanced training. I, too, as part of my mission, will soon establish a Yoruba Temple here in New Orleans in both the Haitian and Yoruba rites. When I was young, and my mother introduced the use of candles and oils . . . even then there was some organization to our beliefs. A wonderful man, Dr. William James, a preacher and in my mind a powerful Voodoo doctor, embodied the weaving of Voodoo beliefs and Christian beliefs and influenced my "religion." Because of my time studying in Haiti and living among the population of that far-away country, I have become, and this is important to understand, not a queen but a priestess of Voodoo. The designation Mambo is an accurate one for what I do. And I am initiated in the rites of Yoruba and am a member of the Palo Mayumba Voodoo cult. My training in Haiti was a process of getting myself spiritually straight and then obtaining formal recognition via initiation. It was like being licensed in any of the professions. It's a costly endeavor. I spent some $12,000 becoming a priestess. Still, the Vodun religion insists on this level of determination and competence. (I emphasize my involvement into the Yoruba religion as a priestess of the

Goddess Oya for several reasons. The Yoruba religion is the most widely spread manifestation of the African religions in the world. From it comes Santeria of the New World, Macumba of South America, the Shango Baptists of Trinidad, and the traditional Youlba religion of which I am a part. Secondly, I am very deeply involved with the Yoruba practice. The Haitian Vodun and the Youlba religions can be considered sister religions).

Q: I wonder why a modern person turns not to modern ways but to Voodoo?

AKJ: I've always been interested in my West African heritage. African music and dance intrigue me. In college and even today I'm involved in a cosmopolitan dance ensemble, the Voodoo Macumba Dance Ensemble, and we bring the performance side of Voodoo to the public in hopes of having them better understand what Voodoo is all about . . . So you see I walked away from a possible teaching career and a legal career to help keep alive the traditions I value   from Africa. A tradition that was never completely lost. Even in slavery days when some masters insisted on the Christianization of the black man, slaves simply pretended to accept the master's religion and in a Catholic environment it was simple enough to substitute one of the patron saints for one of the parallel Vodun gods. Instead of overtly revering Shango, the god of war, it was more "acceptable" for the slave to revere St. Barbara, the patron of warriors. African tradition was preserved in that way. I don't want to turn my back on my heritage.

Q: You gave up orthodox career opportunities.

AKJ: I had a calling. Some of the calling was cultural, but most of it was based on my early experiences in the positive occult. I now see my role in life as working with the spirits. There are many spirits of course, and they are not far off. Well my work is to help balance out the spirits. To tilt the scales as it were in favor of good spirit forces.

Q: So you wouldn't engage in the so-called black arts.

AKJ: The dark is not Voodoo: it's cultism. Voodoo is not demonic—the worship of Satan is a contorted offshoot of the rich and beautiful nature-based European tradition. The West African tradition is built on revering the spirits of the ancestors and calling on them for assistance and also dealing with the higher forces whom we call *orisa* (the Haitian equivalent to *loas*). These are the gods and goddesses who are cosmically and metaphysically parts of the God Force. Anyway, when I pass, I want to have lived a good, positive life so that my spirit can be near my family—my son and grandchild—and care for them. I couldn't do that if I engaged in hurtful behavior towards anyone.

Q: Where is Catholicism in all of this?

AKJ: I practice both religions. Both I believe are paths to God and spirits. In both of them you are taught that you will reap what you sow. Voodoo is just a more down to earth religion—it's more earthy. In Voodoo you get energy. For example, potions are scented and the natural aromas affect people. Some attract people and some repel people. That's earthy. Now with this scent, Voodoo combines a blessing, prayer, invocation to the spirits and visualization—a powerful tool in personal growth and goal attainment. [The priestess suddenly stood, walked to the nearby altar, splashed a light-smelling oil into her palms and slowly rubbed with slow circular motions the liquid into her face]. All in all, I feel that Voodoo has the same god force as Christianity or Judaism but sees him in an African perspective. And all religions, I think, have a form of Voodoo. Using forces for good, invoking spirits—that's all part of it.

Q: Who seeks out a Voodoo priestess?

AKJ: All kinds of people. Rich and poor. Many come to New Orleans because of its Voodoo reputation—searching—but they don't know what they are searching for. The curious and the hate-filled I have no time for. Some who seek me out are simply psychologically fixated. They feel "crossed." Any (helping professional) could help them. Others are suffering from self-fulfilling prophecies and deep-seeded and long-term negative thinking. But the true cases of "crossing"—the ones where errant or vagrant spirits (deep level demon forces) are involved, require specialized training—the kind that the Voodoo practitioner gets in the Haitian or Yoruba system. Most of the people who see me though are more interested in improving their finances, advancing their careers, and finding and holding on to love. These latter problems make up the business of Voodoo—they constitute the day-to-day reality the practitioner deals with.

Q: You mentioned the business aspect of Voodoo.

AKJ: Voodoo is everything in my life. It's my religion. It's also my work. It is a business that has to be cultivated in that people can only make use of my powers if they can locate me and I can only afford to devote my life to the practice if some remuneration is involved.

Q: Finally, how about misconceptions people hold towards Voodoo?

AKJ: Voodoo is nothing to be feared. If you live a good life and don't hurt others, you have nothing to worry about. Anyway, Voodoo is not a negative. It's a force for good and I use the force and explain the force in my lectures (often to those involved in the medical profession) and in my practice. My work is to spread the reality of Voodoo and to bury the myths that surround it. My life is dedicated to those ends.

As I left the interview, a few thoughts raced through my head. Relying on nature—on whatever's out there to explain the world and to help us survive difficult times is a traditional way of coping with life. When life's pressures become too much, we still head for the mountains, the shore, the seclusion of a warm and cozy den far from the maddening crowds and there nature comforts us, sedates, leads us out of our tumult. Nature had the same effect on people a hundred, a thousand years ago. Jones may well be the sedative some need today to cope with life.

A Hoodoo Find

Sheriff Charles Fuselier of the St. Martin Parish sheriff's office is often kidded by colleagues who refer to him as the "spook's" sheriff. It seems that the sheriff has long been acquainted with the existence of Hoodoo practices in the area. Though still a young man, the sheriff recalls members of his own family in the late 1940s seeking out the Hoodoo practitioner, Marie Pitre, in Breaux Bridge, La. The St. Martin Parish area is rich in Hoodoo folklore.

An engineering school graduate, now the chief law enforcement officer for his rural parish, Sheriff Fuselier some years ago noticed the Hoodoo-like altars—resembling the kinds he had been told about as a youngster—in the cells of Cuban inmates housed in his parish jail.

Santeria, the Cuban Voodoo equivalent, practiced in Cuban-Hispanic populated communities throughout the Americas, fascinated Fuselier. Readings, seminars, and workshops followed and provided a wealth of information, and the sheriff by all accounts is now regarded as one of the most knowledgeable law enforcement officials on Voodoo, Hoodoo and Santeria in Louisiana.

Despite his early glimpses into the world of Hoodoo and despite the knowledge acquired on Santeria, the sheriff had never come face-to-face with a self-professed Hoodoo practitioner. Not until September 15, 1989.

On that date, a criminal investigation unit was dispatched to a typical-looking house on an ordinary street in one of South Louisiana's commonplace rural communities. As soon as the sheriff arrived at the house in Breaux Bridge, his recollections, his studies...led to a hunch. This was no ordinary house. This was the home of a Hoodooist.

Police officers gathered around the body of a nude female thrown from her doorway onto the hood of a parked automobile by the impact of bullet on flesh—the victim shot to death by her estranged lover.

The sheriff scanned the area and as with a jigsaw puzzle put together parts to create a whole picture—parts that individually meant little but parts that when pieced together established the crime scene as a Hoodoo practitioner's "temple."

In the front yard of the residence stood a Catholic statue. But looking up the steps that led to the bungalow, jarred between door and frame, Fuselier spied a curtain drape—Hoodooists in the area routinely hang curtains at each door hoping to prevent the entry of evil, vagrant spirits.

The sheriff entered the small, wood-framed house. Each room was littered with "holy" pictures and prayers glued to walls. Above the doorway were what appeared hand-etched crucifixes. Above one door—opening to a room that led to the back door (the location of the shooting) was nailed a gris gris bag—a good luck charm.

A small aluminum (wash-stand) altar in the same area of the house featured dozens of saint's pictures plastered above the "sacred" table. On the altar was a white Buddha incense burner—a Hoodoo staple; sandwiched between bricks were sheets of note paper with the scribbled names of people to be crossed or uncrossed; also on the home-made altar were various candles labeled "Happiness," "Love," and "Luck." Alongside the candles' charred remains were ceramic images of Jesus and the Virgin.

To the right and adjoining the altar were jars filled with herbs and hair and commercially packaged occult potions, sprays, and powders.

Behind the house, hanging from the rafters of a garden shed was a Poche's cracklin' bag containing a human skull that had apparently been unearthed to help the Hoodoo practitioner contact the spirits of the dead.

Sheriff Fuselier had a find—a treasure trove of Hoodoo staples few are ever able to view.

The next few pages are photos taken at the Breaux Bridge Hoodooist's residence that eventful September day.

The Hoodooist's Breaux Bridge home with Catholic statuary. To most passers-by this was a typical Catholic home. But notice the door curtains—a Hoodoo device used to prevent evil spirits from entering a home.

A gris-gris bag placed over the door protected the homeowner from vagrant spirits. The Hoodooist was murdered a few feet from the doorway.

The Hoodoo altar discovered in the victim's home featured pictures of Catholic saints, candles, a Buddha incense burner, and cans containing the ingredients for mojos, conjos, and gris-gris bags—rural Hoodoo staples.

Using any available means for acquiring power, this Hoodooist (like others in the area) purchased how-to-books.

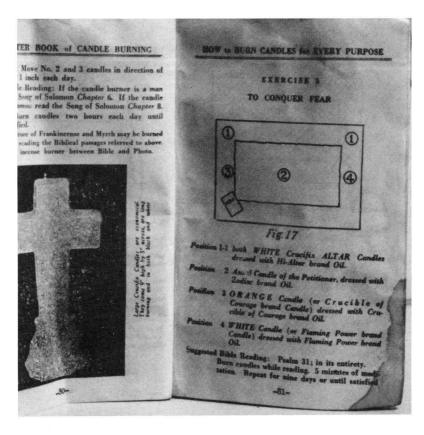

Instructions for burning candles to conquer fear.

The Hoodooist placed orders for these three books.

Placed throughout her home were "prayers" clipped from various sources—all intended to strengthen the practitioner's spells.

Placed in a Poché's cracklin bag, an unearthed skull was used by the Hoodooist to connect with the spirits of the dead. This is another do-it-yourself feature of rural Hoodoo practices.

Closing Remarks

Its origins in the past—in primitive man's attempt to both understand a complex world and to have some modicum of control over life events—Voodoo has evolved.

Born in West Africa, indigenous peoples there explained the world by observing nature and its cycles. Animism! Nature succinctly and simply explained life and death, birth and aging. But it could not impose man's will on events. So man improvised and the Vodu religion was conceived.

Superstition in Europe has a similar pedigree. Getting some handle on life was a rather universal imperative in a constantly changing world. A do-it-yourself approach to obtaining this "mastery" characterized the world of European Satanists, witches, and sorcerers.

With New World slavery the West African Animist tradition and the European world of superstition—both informally organized entities—interacted in a unique milieu. Faced with a hostile and untamed environment, Europeans encountered diseases, storms, swamps; West African slaves endured hostile masters, and both groups needed an "agent" to assist them in controlling their new worlds. The more threatening this world became, the more organized the Voodoo response. Individual Voodoo leaders exercised great freedom in developing this brand of "religion" as had been the case in West African Vodu and European superstition, but the beliefs adopted a more systematic, church-like form in the Americas. Voodoo became the system of superstition most often used for purposes of health and power in Haiti and later in Louisiana and other parts of the U. S.

Today Voodoo persists because man, though richer, freer, and more educated, still from time-to-time feels helpless and hopeless. During such times, what the child and for that matter what our infant species has relied on—the "magical"—provides an out. Voodoo lives where people face desperation and insurmountable odds.

No longer organized, Louisiana Voodoo has evolved into an individualized and splintered set of beliefs, rituals, and superstitions carried on by word of mouth and sought out in the same manner.

Voodoo is a response to man's partial knowledge in a world where the unexpected is to be expected—and often feared!

Glossary of Voodoo Terms as used by Louisiana Informants
(Or What Everbody Should Know About Voodoo)

ancestral altar—seven glasses of water placed in a semi-circle, representing the seven African gods of Vodun. Each of the seven gods has a parallel (patron) saint in Catholicism. NO

animism—a West African belief system emphasizing the worship of spirits both animate and inanimate

arbor church—often constructed of netting on lumber, the structure acted as a meeting place for slaves. Attached to a tree(s) of special significance, it was seen as a magical place and housed secret slave meetings and sings

Buddha bowls—a commercially produced incense burner used in rural Hoodoo since the mid-twentieth century for ritual incense burning. Informants do not know why it is used but they insist on its use in rituals, SWLA

Cajun—a corruption of the word Acadian designating the French inhabitants of Acadia (Nova Scotia) who were exiled from their homes in 1758. A number found their way to southern Louisiana and practiced rural hoodoo.

candles—used in Voodoo and hoodoo rites. Burning different colored candles produces different effects since each color attracts a different patron-spirit. Burning the black candle uncrosses or unhexes.
Other colors and their uses:
Burn red or green candles for prosperity, pink or red for love, white for peace, yellow to attract love, for revenge burn the double-action reversible black candle. For luck, burn candles appropriate to the month of your birth eg. those born in January shoud burn red and gold candles, those born in March should burn blue and gold, those born in June should burn red and blue, and those born in December should burn red and orange candles, LA

Candlemas—Feb.2, obseved as a church festival commerating Christ's presentation in the temple and the purification of the Virgin Mary. The date is considered a significant source of power to some Voodoo practitioners especially if born on that date., NO

charm—any object that a Voodoo practitioner calls on the spirits to possess and thus is embodied with magical powers, NO Good luck charms are worn and malevolent charms are concealed on the victim's person or premises, SWLA

chicken bones—used in hoodoo as an agent for calling evil spirits to do one's bidding, SMP

coffin—a small casket-looking box used as a crossing mechanism and left on the victim's doorway to help usher in evil spirits, NO

Congo Square—known today as Louis Armstrong Park in New Orleans—originally a tract of land set aside for slaves and other blacks to congregate under the watchful eye of the city authorities. Initially these meetings were informal and slaves sang African songs accompanied by hand made instruments replicating those used in their pre-slavery African days

congris—a stew eaten at nineteenth-century Voodoo rituals consisting of black eyed peas, rice, and sugar

conjo (in hoodoo), mojo (in Voodoo)—a bag containing herbs, hair, etc. used to cast a spell, VP

conjure—the act of creating a spell via any agent for calling in the spirits

crossing-the successful calling of a negative power or spirit to inflict harm or bad luck, LA

cure all—the favorite is Jamestown weed, sulphur and honey, sipped from a glass which has been rubbed against a black cat with one white foot, NO

Dahomey—West African slave trading tribe that subjugated the Ewes and helped transport Animism to Haiti

divination—the ability to see into the future and the past, NO

double (or ghost)—the second entity which constitutes each person or thing in nature. The double is usually freed at the time of death and can be called on for assistance. Trees and objects that in some way have doubles eg. a branch growing into another branch are considered powerful and make potent charms, NI

Dr. John—John Montenet, Haitian-born New Orleans Voodoo practitioner who is believed to have first integrated traditional Voodoo ways with elements of Catholicism and the snake oracle

effigy—a likeness of a person often seen on Voodoo dolls and used to call the spirits to assist or harm the person it is fashioned after

errant or vagrant spirits—a Voodoo name for evil spirits who cause mischief or destruction and who can only be exorcised by a Voodoo practitioner, NO

Ewes—a West African tribe noted for its animist beliefs and use of a python diety and who were sold into slavery and transported to the West Indies

extension—usually a piece of clothing or body hair belonging to a person who is to be crossed or uncrossed

feathers—waving them in one's face leads to good luck for gamblers, or a stomach ache depending on the practitioner's intent, NI

fetish—any object believed to have been endowed with magical powers— any charm. Made from alligator teeth, grains, cords with knots, nail-clippings, hair, graveyard dirt or dust, bones, garlic, etc.

feux follet—night lights that cause one to get lost in journey. Sometimes believed to be the searching souls of unbaptized infants and according to others the soul of the evil John who crucified Satan, and banished from hell, was exiled to wander the earth as a ball of fire, SWLA

fixation—a false belief (of psychological origins) wherein one feels crossed, NO

folklore—the unofficial, unrecorded traditions, beliefs, and ways of a people

god—to the Voodooist, a general concept akin to the concept of nature and thus difficult to worship

gods—to the animist many spirits existed and modern Voodoo believes seven are present and each has an equivalent in Catholic patron saints eg. Elegg is a parallel entity to St. Antony, the door opener. Three sets of gods are most revered—the dead, spirits of dead twins, and the loas-messenger gods

gris-gris—from the French word for gray—a potion or conjo to ward off bad luck or to cross another. Often a bag filled with hair, nail-clippings, etc., VP

gros-bon-ange—one of man's two Voodoo souls. It is responsible for animating man's body Ti-Z-Ange—the second of man's two souls. Responsible for protecting against dangers by day and by night (Haiti)

Haiti—Hispanola—West Indies— An island nation located between southeast North America and northern South America bordering the Caribbean and comprising the Greater Antilles. The birthplace of New World Voodoo

headless man—legendary powerful "double" who causes difficulties to anyone spying the headless form, IP

herb doctor (or root doctor)—an African healer who uses nature and its products to treat ailments of various kinds, NO

High John the Conq(uer) root—a root sold in local pharmacies and used in hoodoo and Voodoo rites to obtain the assistance of High John, protector of blacks, NI

incense—burned to help call the correct spirit to the Voodoo (practitioner's) use, VP

Karma—the force generated by a person's actions in Hinduism or Buddhism to perpetuate transmigration and its consequences to determine his destiny in his next existence. Some modern Voodoo practitioners incorporate elements of Karma in their belief system, NO

loa—intermediaries that carry man's messages to god. Major loas are seen as geniuses; minor loas are viewed as spirits

Loup-Garou—a French version of the were-wolf legend, NO

Maison Blanche—the home Marie Laveau built near Lake Pontchartrain and believed to be a popular brothel

mambo—an order of (female) priesthood in the Haitian Vodun religion. She usually has a following of her own in Voodoo's individual approach to religion. NO

Milneburg—now known as Pontchartrain Beach and site of Laveau's Maison Blanche (brothel)

mulatto—first generation offspring of a negro and a white—often associated with the leadership of Voodoo/hoodoo in Louisiana

novenas—(a Catholic nine day devotion for an intention) used as one of many Voodoo/hoodoo means to lead the dead's soul away from earth and thus protecting survivors from the soul's meddling or worse

priestess—one who is formally initiated into a Voodoo rite as practitioner, NO

possession—Voodoo belief that the gods communicate via dreams and by incarnating themselves into a human who then takes on that diety's traits

potions—usually an oil (or some liquid) used as a charm, NO

prayers—said in combination with the use of a charm to produce a powerful Voodoo/hoodoo effect. For example, this prayer has been used when lighting a Voodoo candle: May this offering, I pray thee, O Lord, both loose the bonds of my sins, and win the gift of thy blessed mercy. It is followed by the request for a favor, NO

priests (Voodoo)—have the power to call the gods into jars where the gods converse with those who wish to question them

red rosary beads—used by Voodoo/hoodoo believers to ward evil spirits from the remains of a deceased believer. The beads are placed in the deceased person's hands, I&SMP

Santeria—a Hispanic (expecially Cuban) version of Voodoo, NO

shroud—purple cheesecloth draped over the face of a deceased person in order to ward off evil spirits, IP

snake—the Voodoo oracle used in Laveau's time to inspire the priestess into speaking with the lips of the spirits, NO

Storyville—famous New Orleans brothel district and home to a number of Voodoo priestesses

tafia—a mixture of molasses and rum often consumed at nineteenth-century Voodoo rituals, NO

tongues—animal tongues laced with pins and often "planted" near a tomb to tap into the powers of deceased spirits, NO

uncrossing—a counter agent designed to free a crossed individual. In the hoodoo tradition it consists of praying, incensing, and speaking in unknown tongues, BB

Van Van incense—the rural hoodoo incense used in uncrossing. The incense is commercially available and packed in Chicago, NI

Voodoo—a mix of superstitions with West African animist roots that developed in the West Indies and in the United States, NI hoodoo—the rural corruption of Voodoo in the southern United States, NI

Voodoo gods—consisting primarily of loas, twins, and the dead. Also the old African gods and the spirits of the deceased and of deceased priests and priestesses, and an array of subdieties. Examples of the pantheon:

Agwe—presides over the seas and ships

Bade—loa of the winds

Domballah-Wedo—serpent god

Ezili—personification of feminine grace

Legba—remover of barriers, protector of homes

Loco—spirit of vegetation

Sembi—guardian of fountains and marshes

Sogbu—god of lightning

Zoka—minister of agriculture

Zombi—Voodoo snake diety in the southern United States, NO

Informant Location Code

AP, Acadia Parish   SMP, St. Mary Parish

VP,Vermilion Parish   IP,Iberia Parish
BB, Breaux Bridge
LA, various Louisiana locations
NI, New Iberia
NO, New Orleans
SWLA, Southwest Louisiana

BIBLIOGRAPHY

Amelquist, David. *Hoodoo and Voodoo Today.* Collection no. 168, Patricia Rickels Folklore Collection, Doucet Hall, Rm. 205, University of Southwestern Louisiana, 1969.

Blassingame, John W. *The Slave Community: Plantation Life in the Antebellum South.* London: Oxford University Press, 1979.

Brandon, Elizabeth. "Superstitions in Vermilion Parish." *The Golden Log.* Dallas: SMU Press, 1962, 110-117.

Brasseaux, Carl A. "French Louisiana's Senegambian Legacy," in *Senegal: Peinteur Narratives.* Lafayette: University of Southwestern Louisiana Art Museum, 1986, pp. 56-58.

_____. "The Administration of Slaves in French Louisiana," *Louisiana History,* XXI (1980), 115-42.

Brunvand, Jan. *The Study of American Folklore.* New York: W. W. Norton & Co., 1986.

Castellanos, H. C., *New Orleans As It Was: Episodes of Louisiana Life.* New Orleans: L. Graham and Sons, Ltd., 1895.

Colligan, Douglas. "Extreme Psychic Trauma is the Power Behind Voodoo Death," *Science Digest,* LXXX (1976), 44-48.

Courlander, Harold. *A Treasury of Afro-American Folklore.* New York: Crown Publishing Co., 1976.

Confidential Interview with a Louisiana Hoodoo observer and practitioner: Notes deposited in Southwestern Archives, University of Southwestern Louisiana, Lafayette, Louisiana, April 30, 1990.

Desossiers, Touissant. "Haitian Voodoo," *Americas,* XX (1970), 35-39.

Dorson, Richard M. *Buying the Wind.* Chicago: University of Chicago Press, 1964.

Hall, Gwen R. *Social Control in Slave Plantation Societies.* Baltimore: Johns-Hopkins University Press, 1971.

Harris, Marvin. "Voodoo Death," *Psychology Today*, XVIII (1984), 16-17.

Historical Sketch Book and Guide to New Orleans. New York: W. H. Coleman, 1885.

Le Code Noir, ou, édit du roy, servant de réglement, pour le gouvernment & l'administration de la justice, police, discipline & le commerce des esclaves negres, dans la province & colonie de la Louisianne. Donné à Versailles au mois de mars, 1724. Paris, 1726.

Martinez, Raymond. *Laveau: Voodoo Queen, and Folktales along the Mississippi.* New Orleans: Hope Publishing, 1956.

Metreaux, Alfred. *Voodoo in Haiti.* New York: Oxford University Press, 1959.

Newell, W. M., "Myths of Voodoo Worship and Sacrifice in Haiti," *Journal of American Folklore*, I (1888), 16-30.

Nott, G. W. "Marie Laveau." *New Orleans Times-Picayune*, November 9, 1922, Magazine Section., 2.

Owen, Mary A. "Among the Voodoos," Proceedings of the *International Folk Lore Congress*, (1891), p. 230.

Puckett, Niles. *Folk Beliefs of the Southern Negro.* Chapel Hill: University of North Carolina Press, 1926.

The Picayune Guide to New Orleans. (New Orleans: Nicholson & Co., 1891).

Rawick, George P., "From Sundown to Sunup: The Making of the Black Community," *The American Slave: A Composite Autobiography,* (Westport Ct.: Greenwood Publishing Co., 1972).

"Records of the Superior Council of Louisiana," *Louisiana Historical Quarterly*, II (1919)-XXVI (1943).

Rhodes, Jewell Parker. "Marie Laveau," *Ms. Magazine*, XI (1983), 28-31.

Rickels, Patricia K. "The Folklore of Sacraments and Sacramentals in South Louisiana," *Louisiana Folklore Miscellany,* (1965), 27-44.

Schick, Tom. "Healing and Race in the South Carolina Low Country," in *Africans in Bondage.* Madison: University of Wisconsin Press, 1986.

Seymour, W. H. "A Voudou Story," *New Orleans Times-Picayune,* July 3, 1892.

Simpson, George Eaton. *Black Religions in the New World.* New York: Columbia University Press, 1978; 51-70.

Taylor, Joe Gray. *Negro Slavery in Louisiana.* New York: Negro Univesity Press, 1963.

Tallant, Robert. *Voodoo in New Orleans.* New Orleans: Pelican Press, 1983.

"Voodoo Kills by Despair," *Science News Letter* 67(1955), 294.

Weld, Theodore Dwight. *American Slavery As It Is: Testimony of a Thousand Witnesses.* New York, 1983.